CRICKET

CRICKET

CRICKET
The Essentials of the Game

Sir Richard Hadlee

Swankit
Division of India Research Press

Swankit
India Research Press
B-4/22, Safdarjung Enclave,
New Delhi – 110 029.
Ph.: 24694610; Fax : 24618637
bahrisons@vsnl.com
contact@indiaresearchpress.com
www.indiaresearchpress.com

Copyright © Sir Richard Hadlee

2004

South Asia edition © India Research Press, New Delhi

Issued Under Licence from Reed Publishing (NZ) Ltd.

ISBN : 81-87943-45-9

All rights reserved by publisher. No part of this publication, may be reproduced, stored in or introduced into a retrieval system or transmitted in any form, or by any means, electronic, mechanical, photocopying, recording or otherwise, without the prior written permission of the publisher of this book..

Cataloguing in Publication Data
Sir Richard Hadlee
Cricket : The Essentials of the Game
Sir Richard Hadlee

1. Cricket 2. Sports 3. Author 4 . Title

ISBN : 81-87943-45-9

Printed at Focus Impressions, New Delhi – 110 003.

DEDICATION

*To all those who want to learn, play,
appreciate and understand the great game of cricket*

Preface

I have been involved with cricket for many years, from the days when I was a youngster dreaming about playing at the highest level, to becoming the first bowler in the history of the game to capture 400 test wickets.

Cricket has been a wonderful part of my life and I have thoroughly enjoyed what the game has offered me. To have represented my country, to have toured the world, to have served New Zealand Cricket during one of our finest eras, the 1980s, and to have made many friendships are all things of which I am very proud. I have been involved in radio and television commentary and I write newspaper columns about the game.

In 2000 I was appointed chairman of the New Zealand Cricket selection panel and I am now involved in coaching fast bowlers at the High Performance Centre (Academy) near Christchurch.

During my career I have come to appreciate how skilful the game of cricket is, and how mentally tough and physically fit the players must be. They need to be aware of the job they have to do within the team and accept the challenges and the responsibilities involved.

From the excitement of the one-day game to the subtleties of a five-day test match, cricket caters for different types of supporters and spectators. Some people join in the hype of the one-day game, while others appreciate the finer technicalities of a test, even though the result may only be a draw.

The game may look quite easy but when you try to participate, you find there's plenty to know and learn if you want to be successful. Fitness, technique, skill, eyesight, attitude and tactical awareness are all important.

Some claim to find the game complex and boring; unless

you know what is going on, then it will be difficult to enjoy. This book is designed so that everyone can understand cricket in its simplest terms. Some of the information may seem very basic and repetitive, but there are aspects that need to be explained. It is also important to understand the basic Laws of Cricket, the terminology that applies to the game and the phrases used by the commentators. There are tips for players, captains, coaches, parents and spectators that may be helpful and a section on up-to-date world and New Zealand test and one-day records. When rain stops play there is a trivia quiz to test your knowledge of the game.

    I hope this book increases your enjoyment and understanding of the game.

Richard Hadlee

CONTENTS

Preface — vii

Chapter 1 A Brief History of Cricket — 1
Chapter 2 Types of Cricket — 9
Chapter 3 The Pitch — 13
Chapter 4 Fielding Positions — 19
Chapter 5 Bowling — 22
Chapter 6 Batting — 35
Chapter 7 Dismissals — 43
Chapter 8 Teamwork and Training — 47
Chapter 9 The Role of the Captain — 55
Chapter 10 Coaching — 62
Chapter 11 Tips for Parents and Grandparents — 69
Chapter 12 Spectator Etiquette — 72
Chapter 13 Commentators — 75
Chapter 14 Umpires and Match Referees — 89
Chapter 15 How the Game is Scored — 102
Chapter 16 Personal and Team Equipment — 107
Chapter 17 Administrations and Trophies — 113
Chapter 18 Major Cricket Venues — 119
Chapter 19 For the Record — 122
Chapter 20 Cricketing Terms — 137
Chapter 21 Cricket Trivia — 215

CHAPTER 1

A Brief History of Cricket

The first reference to cricket was in 1478, when a game called criquet was played at St Omer in the north-east of France. In 1598 John Derrick claimed he played a game of krickett in England, but it wasn't until 1646 that the first game of cricket was played, when two teams took part at Coxheath in Kent. In 1709 the first match between two English county teams took place, when Kent and Surrey began a rivalry that has lasted nearly 300 years. That same year, 1709, a game of cricket had also been recorded in North America, when William Byrd played a match with friends.

The game of cricket needed some rules, so in 1744 the Laws of Cricket were established. The first women's match was recorded the same year. Women eventually became the first cricketers to bowl overarm; in the early days, underarm bowling was the norm.

The first century to be recorded was by John Small of Hambledon, when he scored 135 against Surrey in 1775. A century was, and still is, regarded as the ultimate achievement for a batsman. For a bowler, a bag of five wickets in an innings is the milestone.

A significant piece of cricket history took place in 1787. Thomas Lord of the White Conduit Club was asked to find a new ground when the club's fields at Islington in London were closed. The new site was on what is now known as Dorset Square, near Marylebone Station. In the same year, the White Conduit Club dissolved and reformed as the Marylebone Cricket Club (MCC), which had the responsibility for governing all cricket until 1969. In 1810, when the lease of the ground had expired. Lord was asked to find another ground on the North Bank of the Thames. Within three years, Lord found another ground only a few hundred metres away to the north-east and in 1814 Lord's Cricket Ground was opened on its present site. Each time the ground was moved, Lord dug up and transplanted the original turf.

In 1859 the first overseas tour took place, when an All England XI under the captaincy of George Parr toured Canada and the United States. That was the start of international cricket, although Canada and the United States had been playing against each other since 1844.

As the game developed, people wanted to know more about cricket, so in 1864 John Wisden started his now famous *Almanack*, in which he recorded match results and other useful information. County cricket was properly constituted the same year but it wasn't until 1890 that an official points system was established to determine the county champions.

The first official test match took place when England played Australia at the Melbourne Cricket Ground (MCG) on 15 March 1877; Australia won. Since then, other international teams have joined the test arena at different times: South Africa in 1889, the West Indies in 1928, New Zealand in 1930, India in 1932, Pakistan in 1952, Sri Lanka in 1982, Zimbabwe in 1992 and finally Bangladesh in 2000.

One-day cricket began in England in 1963, when county teams played for the Gillette Cup. It wasn't until 1971, however, when a test match between England and Australia was abandoned due to bad weather, that the first one-day international was played. On 5 January 1971, Australia beat England by five wickets. In 1975 the West Indies won the inaugural World Cup when they beat the Australians at Lord's.

Cricket has had its controversial moments, and there are five key incidents that have forced changes to the game: the 'bodyline' series, the Packer Series, the underarm incident and, in more recent times, bowlers accused of throwing and, sadly, match fixing and bribery allegations.

Australia's Don Bradman had completely dominated England's bowlers in 1930 when he scored 974 runs at an average of 139.14, including 334 at Headingley. Douglas Jardine, the England captain, knew that Bradman was going to be a threat on the tour of Australia that was to follow. He therefore instructed his battery of fast bowlers, headed by Nottinghamshire's Harold Larwood, to bowl at the batsmen's bodies, with fielders positioned in the leg trap to get them out and prevent them from scoring runs. The plan worked: England won the series 4-1 and Bradman's batting average was reduced to 56.67. The Australian Board of Control was outraged and cabled the MCC, protesting that their 'bodyline' tactics were unsportsmanlike. Bodyline was outlawed and Larwood never played for England again.

On I February 1981, New Zealand was playing Australia in a one-day match at the MCG. New Zealand needed six runs from the last ball to tie the match and force an extra match to decide the series. As Brian McKechnie settled down to face the last ball from

Trevor Chappell, there was a consultation between the latter and his brother and captain, Greg. The umpires then advised McKechnie that the last ball would be bowled underarm, which would deny the batsman any chance of hitting the ball for six. Australia won the match but Greg Chappell, who had instructed his brother to bowl underarm, was condemned worldwide for his unsportsmanlike decision, which breached the spirit of fair play. New Zealand's Prime Minister, Rob Muldoon, said, 'It was appropriate that the Australians were dressed in yellow. It was an act of cowardice.' The rules allowed for underarm bowling, but no one thought that option would be exercised. From that point on, underarm bowling in one-day cricket was banned.

In 1977 the introduction of World Series Cricket (WSC) revolutionised the game. Business tycoon Kerry Packer contracted the world's leading players by offering them large financial inducements to play in Australia each year for three years. Packer changed the game by introducing floodlit games, coloured clothing, a white ball, stump microphones and black sight-screens. Teams from Australia, the West Indies and the Rest of the World competed in the World Series. Better television techniques and the use of extra cameras added a new dimension for viewers and raised the profile of the game.

While the Packer WSC was being played, his contracted players had been banned from official matches by their respective countries. Test and one-day international cricket continued without many of the star players and some countries fielded second-rate teams with the players they had available. Clearly, the game could not survive for either party, so peace and common ground were found. In 1979, all 'rebel' players were reinstated.

In 1999, at Adelaide, umpire Ross Emerson no balled Muttiah

Muralitharan, the Sri Lankan off-spinner, for throwing. On the previous Sri Lankan tour of Australia, Muralitharan was no balled on many occasions. Emerson was one of the umpires who had been involved during the previous tour. The International Cricket Council (ICC) set up a panel to make a ruling from video footage supplied. Their verdict was that Muralitharan's action was a legal delivery.

During the 1999 Adelaide incident, Arjuna Ranatunga, the Sri Lankan captain, and his players walked to the boundary and play was halted for 12 minutes while administrators discussed the situation. Play later recommenced, but Murali's action continued to be the centre of attention. (Other bowlers have also had their action scrutinised by an independent judging panel.)

The game's greatest crisis came to a head in 2000. For years rumours had circulated that some players were accepting bribes to fix the results of matches. Former players and team mates began making public comments suggesting these actions were rife. But shock waves were sent throughout the cricketing world when allegations were made against Hanse Cronje, the South African captain, whose reputation until then had been impeccable. He had been implicated and later admitted to giving information to an Indian bookmaker about pitch and weather conditions, although he denied fixing match results. The United Cricket Board of South Africa immediately sacked Cronje, both as captain and from the team, for giving information and accepting money. The ICC reacted by launching a worldwide investigation in an effort to eliminate this 'virus' from the game and imposed severe penalties on any player convicted of such crimes. Life bans became mandatory and it was suggested that their playing records be erased from the record books as they no longer had any credibility.

Playing gear and equipment has changed over the years. Players used to wear three-cornered hats covered with silver and gold lace. Breeches, coat, silk stockings and buckled shoes eventually made way for white flannel trousers, shirts and peaked caps, although sunhats are very common today. Club and international colours, which clearly identify the teams, were introduced for one-day matches in 1976.

The cricket bat used to be rounded and similar to a hockey stick. Scooping the ball was easy but it was difficult to hit the ball straight. Today the bat has a flat, open blade with a handle and a rubber grip, allowing the ball to be hit in any direction.

Originally, two stumps, or pieces of stick, 12 inches (30.48 centimetres) high, were positioned 6 feet (1.83 metres) apart. A third stump was introduced in 1775. Two bails, which rested across the top of the stumps, were introduced to the game around 1785. In 1931 a change was made to the dimensions, with the stumps now 28 inches (71.1 centimetres) high and 9 inches (22.86 centimetres) apart. These dimensions are still in use today.

Cricket has been blessed with many great players, some of whom have been accorded legendary status. Dr. William Gilbert Grace of Gloucestershire and England, known as W.G., is perhaps the greatest cricketer of all time. The bearded all-rounder scored 54,896 runs, at an average of 39.55, including 126 centuries, and he captured 1876 wickets at an average of 17.92. Australia's Sir Donald Bradman was the master batsman, with 6,996 test runs at an average of 99.94 runs per innings. West Indian Sir Garfield Sobers is still regarded as the modern day's greatest all-rounder with 8,032 test runs at an average of 57.78, including 26 centuries. He also captured 235 test wickets at an average of 34.03 runs per wicket, and took 109 catches. Wilfred Rhodes, England's left- arm bowler, is still the most successful wicket taker of all time, with 4187 first-class wickets.

'Fiery' Fred Trueman, the Yorkshire and England fast bowler, became the first bowler to capture 300 test wickets on 15 August 1964. He said that if anyone beat his record, 'they would be bloody tired'. By 1998, 13 bowlers had surpassed the 300 test wicket milestone. Trueman became one of the genuine characters in the game during the 1950s and 1960s.

The 1970s and 1980s were dominated by the West Indies. Their match-winning fast bowlers and attacking batsmen destroyed opposing teams. Viv Richards, who later became Sir Vivian Richards, was the master batsman during that time, but Australia's Dennis Lillee was perhaps regarded as the world's best ever fast bowler, with a world record 355 test wickets. All-rounders Imran Khan (Pakistan), Ian Botham (England), Kapil Dev (India) and Richard Hadlee (New Zealand) were dominant for their countries and had many fascinating battles against each other. In 1994, Kapil Dev became the world's greatest test wicket taker, with 434 wickets, however, West Indian fast bowler Courtney Walsh now leads the way with nearly 500 test wickets — a remarkable achievement. Allan Border of Australia has scored more test runs than anyone else, with 11,174 runs at an average of 50.56. By the time Border retired in the 1990s, Graham Gooch of Essex and England had scored more runs than anyone else with over 65,000 runs in all forms of cricket, including test, first-class and one-day.

Currently, India's Sachin Tendulkar is regarded as the best batsman in the world, and he is likely to go on and break most batting records in test and one-day cricket. West Indian Brian Lara and Australia's Steve Waugh also dominate the batting scene. South Africa's fast bowler Allan Donald, Pakistan's Shoaib Akhtar and Australia's Brett Lee and leg-spinner Shane Warne are causing batsmen plenty of problems.

Cricket was introduced to the Commonwealth Games for the first time in 1998. The inaugural gold medal was won by South Africa, with the silver medal going to Australia and the bronze to New Zealand. The game is still undergoing changes, with other forms of cricket being played — indoor, Cricket Max, eight-a-side and six-a-side tournaments. Perhaps one day there will be a world championship of cricket to determine the world's best test-playing nation.

At the beginning of the new millennium an independent panel of administrators, former players and journalists selected their greatest players of the twentieth century. Wisden 2000 lists the top ten as:

1. Sir Donald Bradman
2. Sir Garfield Sobers
3. Sir Jack Hobbs
4. Shane Warne
5. Sir Vivian Richards
=6. Dennis Lillee
=6. Sir Frank Worrell
8. Wally Hammond
9. Dennis Compton
=10. Sir Richard Hadlee
=10. Imran Khan

CHAPTER 2

Types of Cricket

Different forms of cricket cater for different types of players and spectators. Some prefer the slower paced test match., while others prefer the games that have more action and excitement such as the one-day or day-night match.

TEST CRICKET

This is an international match between two teams of II players from two different countries. There are ten major test-playing countries — Australia, Bangladesh, England, India, New Zealand, Pakistan, South Africa, Sri Lanka, the West Indies and Zimbabwe. The game is played over a period of five days and both teams will have two innings each. A minimum of 90 overs must be bowled in a day's play and a minimum of 15 overs has to be bowled in the scheduled last hour of play on the final day. Batsmen have plenty of time to build an innings and score runs, with a century being the ultimate goal.

Bowlers can bowl any number of overs in a match without restriction and if a bowler captures five or more wickets in an innings, he has been very successful. A match is won when the team batting second has scored more runs than the opposition, or if the team bowling last has captured 10 of the batting team's wickets. If the team batting last has not scored the necessary runs and has not lost 10 wickets, then the match is a draw. On rare occasions, a match can be tied when the team batting last has scored the same number of runs as the opposition and lost its tenth wicket when the total runs over both innings are the same.

FIRST-CLASS CRICKET

This type of match is played between two teams of 11 players from two different provinces, states or counties. The match usually lasts three or four days. When an international team tours another country and plays against a provincial team, the match is deemed to be a first-class game. The game is similar to the test match format.

ONE-DAY CRICKET

This form of cricket consists of two teams of 11 players playing a limited overs match, usually 50 overs. There are many restrictions. The team bowling first has to bowl the 50 overs within a certain period of time, usually three and a half hours. No bowler can bowl more than 10 overs during the innings. There are fielding restrictions, with only two men positioned outside a 30-metre circle for the first 15 overs. After that period a minimum of four players still have to remain inside the circle. In these matches there must be at least two fielders in a stationary catching position, no more than 15 metres from the batsman during the first 15 overs. In countries like England, they used to play 40-over Sunday league matches with similar rules. The team scoring most runs wins the game. There are no draws in this form of cricket, but the match can be tied if the runs are equal, irrespective of wickets lost. A lot of people enjoy this type of game because it is action-packed and there is always a result.

ONE-DAY INTERNATIONAL CRICKET

Two teams of 11 players from two different countries playing a limited overs match, usually 50 overs; in all other ways it is the same as one-day cricket.

EIGHT-A-SIDE

Two teams of eight players, with special rules relating to the number of overs that will constitute a match, what the fielding restrictions will be, and the number of overs any one bowler is permitted to bowl.

SIX-A-SIDE

Two teams of six players, with special rules relating to the number of overs that will constitute a match, what the fielding restrictions will be and the number of overs any one bowler is permitted to bowl.

ONE-DAY DAY-NIGHT CRICKET

This form of the game evolved from Kerry Packer's World Series Cricket in 1977. The 50-over match usually starts at 2.30 p.m. and continues through to 10.15 p.m. under high-powered lights. A white ball is used, there are black sight-screens and the players wear coloured clothing.

CRICKET MAX

This game was developed by former New Zealand cricketer Martin Crowe. It is an action-packed game with special rules to add to the excitement. The match is completed within three and a half hours. This is a two innings match between two teams of II players. Each innings lasts for 10 overs. There is a max zone in front of and to the left and right of the sight-screen at each end. If the batsman hits the ball into the max zone behind the bowler, his score is doubled; e.g. if the ball is hit over the max zone boundary, sixes become 12s, and fours become eights, etc. No fielder is allowed in the max zone until the ball has been bowled. Batsmen are rewarded for hitting the ball straight. Bowlers can only bowl a maximum of four overs in the match — maybe two in each innings or four in one innings. If the bowler bowls a no ball the batsman gets a free hit to the next delivery. Most of these games have been played in New Zealand between the provincial teams, culminating in a final. Many of the games are televised.

DOUBLE-WICKET CRICKET

Two teams of two players play against each other but nine fielders are provided for each team. Special rules apply, i.e. both players would be required to bowl five overs to each other in a match that will last for 10 overs. If a batsman is dismissed, he may be able to keep batting but runs will be deducted from his score. The team batting second would still have to bat the 10 overs to win the match because wickets lost and runs deducted for the loss of wickets will affect the final score and the result. These types of competitions are played around the world and suit the allrounder — a player who can bat and bowl well.

SINGLE-WICKET CRICKET

Similar format to the double-wicket game but it involves only one player playing against another, with 10 fielders being provided for each player. Each player needs to have very good batting and bowling skills to be competitive in this form of cricket,

INDOOR CRICKET

This game, which is very fast and requires some skill, is popular with those who do not play the normal version of cricket outdoors. The game is played inside a net with special rules applying. A special lightweight ball is used, batsmen do not wear protective pads or gloves and they run only half the distance of the pitch.

CHAPTER 3

The Pitch

The game of cricket is usually played on an arena, usually oval, called the cricket field, the field or the field of play. This can be in a park, at a school or a specially developed cricket ground.

The size of ovals will vary depending on the ground space available. Usually, the pitch is centred in the middle of the playing field with the longer (or straight hit) boundaries between 60 and 80 metres from the stumps at each end to the boundary line. The square (or side) boundaries are sometimes a shorter distance from the pitch. This will change depending on which pitch in the playing block is being used for the match in progress.

The pitch, which is also called the wicket, is the area between the bowling creases at each end (Law 7.1) and is prepared in an area known as the playing block. On some grounds, between three and 10 pitches may be prepared from that block. While one pitch is being used, another is being rested, allowing it to recover, while yet another is being prepared for a new match.

The pitch conditions can affect how a player will perform and they often help to dictate the outcome of the match. Over the period of a five-day test or even a three-day first-class match, the pitch will change through use and deterioration, and tactics will vary accordingly.

Ground staff take great pride in the pitch they produce. They spend countless hours preparing and grooming the pitch so that it is fair for both teams. Normally, they like to see a pitch that has some pace and bounce to encourage the faster bowler. The bounce of the ball needs to be consistent, allowing the batsmen to play their shots. As the game progresses, the bounce of the ball may become lower, allowing the batsmen to dominate. Usually, on the last day of a test or first-class match the general wear and tear on the pitch, caused by the bowlers' foot marks, the batsmen running up and down the pitch area and the change in the weather conditions, may allow the spin bowlers to become very effective.

Club pitches are usually prepared by local city council employees. Although they try to prepare a good pitch, sometimes the quality is not up to standard. Because they are often asked to prepare many other pitches for weekend games, they can lack the time to bring one pitch up to the necessary standard. These pitches are often left uncovered so, if it rains the night before the game, it is difficult to get a fair pitch and winning the toss becomes crucial. Long periods of rain or drought may prevent ground staff from preparing the true surface that everyone wants.

Some teams play on artifical pitches that need no preparation. They are also safer for children's and lower grade matches because the surface is consistent.

TYPES OF PITCH

There are seven types of pitch.

A GOOD OR PLUMB PITCH

This pitch has a true and reliable bounce. The batsmen will expect to make runs easily provided they are prepared to occupy the crease. There will be little or no seam for a faster bowler or spin for a spin bowler. The bowler will have to work very hard to get the batsman out because the ball will not deviate. Such a pitch is ideal for one-day cricket.

A GREEN OR GREEN-TOPPED PITCH

This pitch is well grassed, so the seam and faster bowlers will prosper because the ball will move off the seam and create problems for the batsman. If such a pitch is left exposed to the rain, the bowlers will have a decided advantage. The ball will move awkwardly both sideways and upwards. It will leave little indentations on the pitch that will give the bowler a clue as to the length he is bowling and whether he needs to make adjustments.

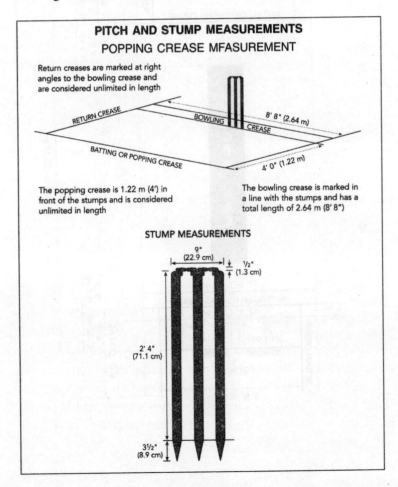

PITCH DIMENSIONS

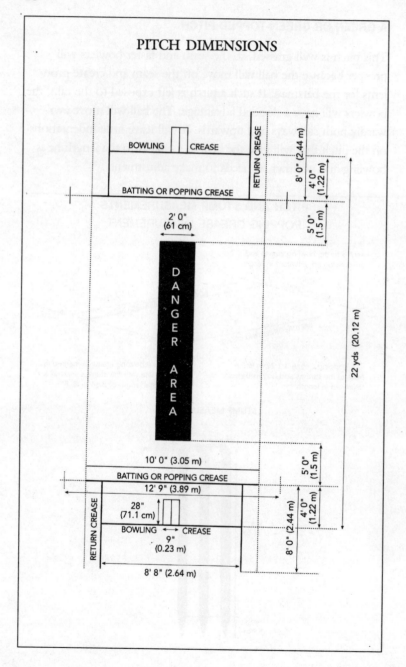

A FAIR PITCH

This pitch creates a good contest between the batsman and the bowler where both can show their skills. Although it may have a greenish look to it before the start of play, there is little or no grass cover. The bounce of the ball is consistent in both height and deviation off the seam and the spin bowler will get some turn or spin as .the match progresses. This type of pitch appears to be rare these days.

A SPORTING PITCH

This type of pitch is likely to deteriorate badly and quickly, usually because it is far too dry. Drought or underwatering can cause the dry, hard soil to crack and, if the ball lands in those cracks, it will bounce unpredictably, allowing the faster bowler to prosper with the uneven bounce. The fast bowlers can be lethal in these sorts of conditions.

A CRUMBLING PITCH

This type of pitch also results from dry conditions and the lack of a binding grass cover. Spin bowlers will prosper in these conditions. The ball is likely to pop, bounce and spin, making it very difficult for the batsman to survive, let alone score runs. Some medium pace bowlers who cut the ball will also profit from such conditions.

A ROUGH PITCH

Although this kind of pitch should never occur, sadly, it does, because no one has taken the time to prepare the pitch properly and spend time cutting, watering and rolling. Sometimes, too, there is misjudgement by ground staff. The end result is that the batsman has no chance of survival and is also likely to be hit by the ball. The ball does not come off the pitch truly, often keeping low, with the next ball jumping at the batsman. Some games have been abandoned because the pitch is too dangerous.

A STICKY WICKET

This pitch has been overwatered or is rain affected. As the pitch starts to dry out in the hot sunshine, the term sticky wicket applies. Batsmen find this type of pitch very difficult to bat on. A crust is formed on the surface, and the ball lifts and/or turns unpredictably. In countries like New Zealand and England, spin and seam bowlers will prosper. In hotter countries like Australia and the West Indies, the faster bowlers tend to reap the benefits.

Spectators can generally tell what sort of pitch is being played on by the position or the placement of the fielders. If the wicket-keeper and the slips are standing well back behind the stumps, then you can assume that the pitch has plenty of pace, bounce and carry. The faster bowlers like to bowl in these conditions.

If the wicket-keeper and only two slips are positioned behind the stumps, then you can assume that the pitch has little or no pace and bounce and that the batsmen will be more difficult to dismiss and will find it easier to score runs.

If a spin bowler is bowling with plenty of close-in fielders, then the pitch is starting to take some spin and survival for the batsmen is much more difficult. Captains always take the condition of the pitch into account when they win the toss. Generally, when a captain wins the toss, he will bat first, provided the pitch looks good. He will take advantage of the pitch being in its best condition, hoping for it to deteriorate for the team batting last.

If the pitch looks as though it will offer the faster bowlers every encouragement, the captain will bowl first to get an early advantage. He will then hope for the batting conditions to be better and easier a little later in the match so he can get a sizeable lead on the first innings and then put the opposition under pressure.

Normally, the golden rule is 'If you *win* the toss, think about putting the opposition in to bat, but then bat first'.

CHAPTER 4

Fielding Positions

Only 11 players can take the field of play at any one time. The wicket-keeper takes up his position behind the wickets at the batsman's end. The bowler bowls from the opposite end, leaving the captain and the bowler to strategically place the other nine fieldsmen in a position to get the batsman out or prevent him scoring runs.

Returning a fielded ball.

Normally a new ball fast bowler will have three slips, a gully, a cover, a mid-off, a mid-on, a silly mid-on (bat-pad) and a fine or long leg in position. As the innings progresses, a slip may come out and be positioned at third man, and the silly mid-on is moved back to square leg.

A first change bowler may have only two slips and a gully, with an extra man positioned in the covers. This is a more defensive field.

A spin bowler can have a very attacking field set if conditions allow: a slip, silly mid-off, short cover, leg gully and short mid-wicket.

If you study the fielding positions diagram, you can see that many different fielding positions are available. It becomes like a game of chess, manipulating and changing the field around depending on match situations, the state of the pitch and how the batsman is playing.

Close-in fielders should be stooped and ready for any catches.

Get your body behind the ball when stopping it

If the pitch is difficult to bat on, and the batsman is struggling or out of form, or you are trying to win a match, then the field placing will be very attacking. If the pitch is playing well, the batsman is on top and you are trying to save the match and draw it, then the fielding positions will become more defensive and widespread.

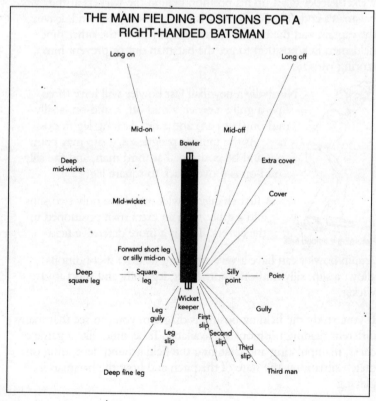

THE MAIN FIELDING POSITIONS FOR A RIGHT-HANDED BATSMAN

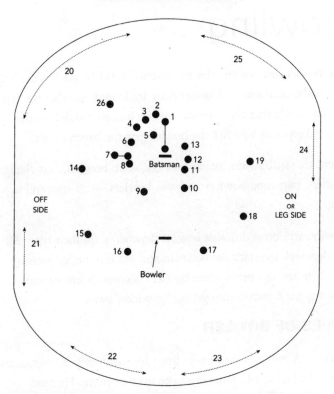

THE MOST GENERAL FIELDING POSITIONS FOR A RIGHT-ARM BOWLER BOWLING TO A RIGHT-HANDED BATSMAN

CLOSE CATCHERS
1. Wicket-keeper
2. First slip
3. Second slip
4. Third slip
5. Short slip
6. Gully
7. Backward point
8. Point
9. Silly mid-off (bat-pad on the off side)
10. Silly mid-on (bat-pad on the leg side)
11. Forward short leg
12. Short leg
13. Backward short leg/ Leg gully

MIDFIELD
14. Cover point
15. Extra cover
16. Mid-off
17. Mid-on
18. Mid-wicket
19. Square leg

OUTFIELD
20. Third man
21. Deep extra cover
22. Long off
23. Long on
24. Deep square leg
25. Fine or long leg
26. Fly slip

CHAPTER 5

Bowling

The bowler dictates the play because wherever he pitches the ball affects the outcome — whether runs are scored, whether the ball is played at, whether the batsman lets the ball go through to the wicket-keeper or whether the bowler gets the batsman out.

There are fast bowlers, swing bowlers, seam bowlers, first change bowlers, part-time bowlers and spin bowlers — off-spin and leg-spin.

Bowlers will bowl different lengths depending on their type. All bowlers seek to attack the batsman and put him under pressure, but there are also times when bowlers become defensive and frustrate the batsman into giving his wicket away.

TYPES OF BOWLER

FAST — A bowler who runs in from approximately 20 metres and bowls the ball at 145 kilometres per hour or more. He tends to rely on extreme pace and is sometimes erratic. A fast bowler tries to unsettle the batsman with intimidation and with a barrage of bouncers. He forces the batsman to hurry his shots with the fast yorker or a lifting ball outside off stump, which is difficult to play. A fast bowler likes pitches that have plenty of pace and bounce, and is lethal on green-topped pitches. He may be required to bowl 16-20 overs in a day in four spells of four or five overs.

FAST MEDIUM — A bowler who usually has more control than the fast bowler but can bowl a quicker ball that can take the batsman by surprise. He may have the ability to swing the ball in the air or cut the ball off the pitch.

MEDIUM FAST — A bowler who tends to bowl within his limits and therefore in long spells. To achieve this he has developed some good skills and many variations — swing, seam, slower, faster balls.

SWING — A bowler who can move the ball in the air, with the seam of the ball being in an upright position. An outswing bowler tends to create more problems for the batsman than an inswing bowler, because the ball goes away or leaves the batsman. A swing bowler enjoys humid conditions because the ball swings more.

SEAM — A bowler who can move the ball off the pitch at a brisk pace. He enjoys pitches that are green and have some bounce.

FIRST CHANGE — After one of the new ball bowlers has finished his spell of around five overs, the first change bowler takes over, usually for a longer spell. He is often a strong person who bowls at a brisk pace, moving the ball in the air or off the seam. He is a stock bowler whose job is to do the donkey work during the day. He may be required to bowl up to 25 overs in a day, with each bowling spell lasting from seven to ten overs at a time. This type of bowler is usually a medium or medium fast paced bowler.

PART-TIME — Usually a specialist batsman who is asked to bowl a few overs to rest the main strike bowlers or to try something different that might break up a successful batting partnership. He could be a medium pace or a spin bowler who may bowl five or six overs in an innings.

OFF-SPINNER — A spin bowler who uses his fingers to spin the ball from left to right or from the off stump to the leg stump

BASIC BOWLING ACTION
Side On

BASIC BOWLING ACTION
Front On

towards the batsman. He tends to flight the ball by giving it plenty of air in an attempt to deceive the batsman and entice him to leave his crease. The bowler needs a pitch that is helpful ecause he relies on spin and bounce. He will try to pitch the ball outside the off stump forcing the drive shot. The arm ball, which is bowled a lot straighter, is bowled at a quicker pace through the air and will swing away from the batsman.

WRIST-SPINNER or LEG-SPINNER — This type of bowler spins the ball from right to left or from the leg stump to the off stump. He can be a match winner if he has the control. This is the hardest ball to bowl because the fingers and the whole wrist are used. Sometimes the ball is dragged down too short and batsmen prosper. If the bowler can consistently pitch the ball in the right area and the pitch is offering assistance, he can get easy wickets. He will also develop other types of deliveries that make him difficult to read, i.e. flipper, wrong 'un (googly/Bosie) or top-spinner. He will generally pitch the ball on the middle stump for the leg-spin delivery, but bowl the ball wider of the off stump for the wrong 'un (ball spins from off to leg).

LEFT-ARM ORTHODOX — This is a left-arm finger-spinner who spins or turns the ball from right to left or from the leg stump to the off stump. He will also have an arm ball that swings in the air towards the batsman.

CHINAMAN — This a very rare type of bowler who bowls slow left arm but, using his fingers and wrist, spins or turns the ball from left to right or from the off stump to the leg stump. It is the left-arm bowler's off-break to a right-handed batsman.

LOB — This type of bowler is rarely seen these days unless someone is playing their first game of cricket and is learning to bowl. The bowler has little or no run-up and lobs the ball into the air so that the end result is usually a very slow delivery, pitched very full; often it is a full toss.

DIFFERENT TYPES OF BALLS BOWLED (TO A RIGHT-HANDED BATSMAN)

OUTSWING — The ball that swings in the air and leaves the batsman. The ball is pitched on or about the middle and off stump, forcing the batsman to play at the ball while the ball moves away towards the slips. Many batsmen are caught out in the slips area. The shinier side of the ball is on the right-hand side or the outside as it leaves the bowler's hand.

INSWING — The ball that swings in the air and angles in towards the batsman. The ball is pitched about 15 centimetres outside the off stump, forcing the batsman to play at it. The shinier side of the ball is on the left-hand side or the inside as it leaves the bowler's hand.

LEG-CUTTER — The seam of the ball is upright as it hits the pitch and deviates away from the batsman towards first slip. Like the outswinger, the ball is pitched on or about the middle and off stump., forcing the batsman to play at it. Another way of seaming the ball is to place the fingers across the seam and pull them down the left-hand side of the ball, getting it to rotate, hit the pitch and move to the left.

OFF-CUTTER — The seam of the ball is upright as it hits the pitch and deviates in towards the batsman. Another way of seaming or cutting the ball is to place the fingers diagonally across the seam of the ball and then pull them down the right-hand side, getting the ball to rotate in the air, hit the pitch and move to the right. The ball is pitched just outside the line of the off stump, forcing the batsman to play at the ball.

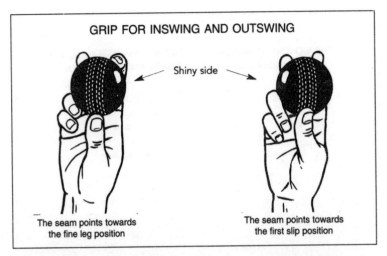

FINGER-SPIN or OFF-SPIN - The ball spins or turns in to the batsman towards leg slip. The ball is pitched outside the line of the off stump, forcing the batsman to play at the ball.

LEFT-ARM ORTHODOX FINGER-SPIN - The ball spins or turns away from the batsman towards first slip. The ball is pitched on or about the middle stump, spinning towards the off stump.

RIGHT-ARM WRIST-SPIN (LEG-SPIN) - The ball spins or turns away from the batsman towards first slip. The ball is pitched on or about the middle and off stump, spinning towards and outside the off stump. On a wearing pitch, with footholes being exploited outside the line of the leg stump, the bowler may alter or change his line according to conditions to extract unpredictable bounce and assistance from the pitch.

CHINAMAN - The ball spins or turns in to the batsman towards leg slip. The ball is pitched outside the off stump.

GOOGLY - A ball that is bowled out of the back of the leg-spinner's hand with a leg-break action, but spins the other way, i.e. spins or turns back in to the batsman towards leg slip. The ball is pitched on or about the off stump. Also known as a Bosie.

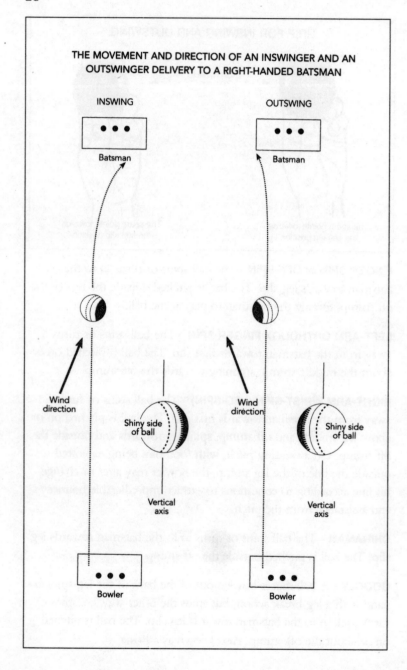

LEG-SPIN AND OFF-SPIN TO A RIGHT-HANDED BATSMAN

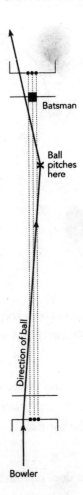

THE LEG-BREAK

– right-arm leg-spinner
– left-arm finger-spinner
– the googly of the left-arm wrist-spinner

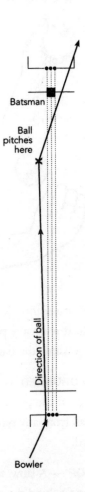

THE OFF-BREAK

– right-arm finger-spinner
– left-arm wrist-spinner
– the googly of the right-arm wrist-spinner

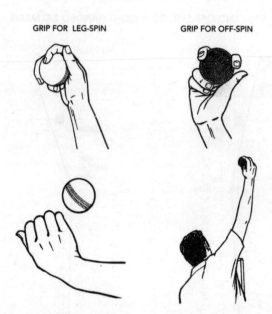

FLIPPER — A leg-spinner's quicker ball that tends to keep low and skids through. It is usually pitched about off stump and may spin or turn back towards the batsman.

SHOOTER or GRUBBER — The ball tends to 'die' or keep very low, not rising off the pitch after it has landed. This is often an unplayable ball from any type of bowler. The batsman can be out, lbw or bowled.

DONKEY DROP — A slow, full delivery that does not pitch and is directed to land behind the batsman and hit the wickets on the full. This delivery is not bowled very often these days. When it is, it usually comes from a lob bowler. If it is badly directed, the batsman will score easy runs.

WRONG 'UN — Another term for the googly. The ball spins back towards the batsman with a leg-spin action.

BOUNCER or BUMPER — A short-pitched delivery from a fast bowler that rises sharply and is directed at the head of the batsman who will try to take evasive action by ducking or swaying out of the way. Umpires are asked to control this type of delivery because it is regarded as unfair play. Some batsmen may attempt to play the hook shot at this type of ball.

BOSIE — See googly.

LOB — See donkey drop.

ARM BALL — Used by an off-spin or left-arm orthodox spin bowler. Instead of trying to spin or turn the ball, he will attempt to swing the ball in the air. An arm ball is normally bowled much more quickly than his spin delivery. The off-spinner's arm ball will swing away from the right-handed batsman; the left-arm orthodox spinner will attempt to swing the ball in towards the right-handed batsman.

TOP-SPIN — Spin that allows the ball to gain pace off the pitch when hitting the ground and then continue on the same line. This type of ball is usually bowled by the leg-break bowler to good effect, although the off-break bowler can bowl them with less success.

BEAMER — This ball should never be bowled because it is a deliberate full toss aimed at the batsman's head and may cause injury. Umpires and match referees are very tough on bowlers who bowl beamers. Sometimes the ball may slip from the bowler's hand and become an unintentional beamer. The bowler will then apologise to the batsman.

VARYING LENGTH

Bowlers will vary their length according to the type of bowler they are, the current pitch conditions and the state of the match. The right length is the one where the ball is pitched to cause the batsman most problems and make it most difficult to score runs. A bowler is likely to bowl six lengths during a spell at the crease.

GOOD LENGTH — The ball is directed on or about the off stump, bringing the batsman, who treats the ball with respect, forward. Few or no runs are scored off these balls.

SHORT OF A LENGTH — The batsman is generally forced onto the back foot to play a defensive shot.

HALF VOLLEY — The ball is pitched nearer the batsman's feet. Batsmen like these deliveries because they are easy to score from, usually being hit for four runs, particularly if the ball is wide of the off stump or overpitched on the leg stump.

YORKER — This is an effective wicket-taking ball. It is generally bowled more quickly by any type of bowler and takes the batsman by surprise. The ball is pitched very full at the batsman's feet and he plays over the top of it, to be out bowled or, if he is fortunate, he may be able to dig the ball out and keep his wicket intact. There is a fine line between bowling an effective yorker and a half volley; some attempted yorkers become full tosses.

LONG HOP — A ball that pitches halfway down the pitch and is considered a gift for easy runs. The ball comes off the pitch slowly and the batsman has plenty of time to get into position and pull the ball for four or six runs. This delivery should be eliminated.

FULL TOSS (FULL 'PEE' or FULL 'BUNGER') — The ball does not pitch and reaches the batsman on the full, normally about waist high. Runs are scored freely from slower bowlers but a fast bowler can take the batsman by surprise. Some full toss deliveries can get wickets, especially if the batsman mistimes a shot and is caught out.

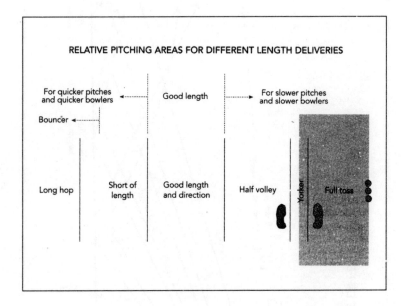

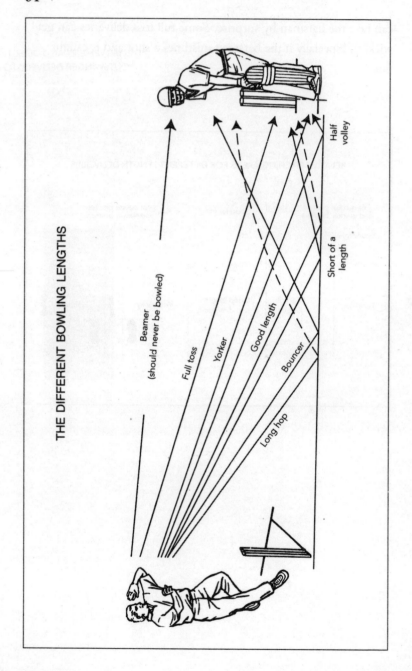

CHAPTER 6

Batting

The batsman's job is to occupy the crease as long as possible, score runs and have a batting approach that is in the best interests of the team. He can score his runs in singles, twos, threes or by hitting boundaries —sixes or fours — where he does not have to run. Sometimes the batsman will benefit from overthrows. Generally speaking, a batsman should be able to score a century, the ultimate batting achievement, in four hours. A batsman can score a century in less than two hours but it will mean taking a lot of risks.

DIFFERENT TYPES OF BATSMEN

DEFENSIVE — A batsman with a solid technique and very good concentration who prefers to occupy the crease for long periods of time, collecting his runs in singles and scoring the odd boundary. He will frustrate the bowler because he takes few risks and will play at balls only if he has to. If he bats for more than four hours, he should have scored 100.

ATTACKING — A batsman who seeks to dominate and stamp his expression and authority on the game as soon as he comes to the crease. He will want to hit boundaries early in his innings and to upset the bowler's line and length. He will take risks, mostly calculated, but in doing so can be vulnerable if he is too impetuous. Bowlers need to vary their pace and make adjustments in the field to upset the rhythm of attacking batsmen.

FRONT-FOOT — A batsman who looks to get well forward to most balls that are bowled. He is trying to eliminate the lbw dismissal. By pushing forward, he is becoming the aggressor, so the bowler has to readjust his length. He is looking to score his runs in front of the wicket with pushes and drives. Most front-foot players enjoy pitches that are low and slow in pace and bounce. Bowlers need to bowl a little shorter to these batsmen to force them onto the crease or back foot.

NB Ideally, a batsman should be proficient off both the front and the back foot. A very good shot to develop is the drive off the back foot, which will place the ball in the area between cover point and wide mid-on. To be fully effective, the weight should be on the rear foot, with the front providing balance. Refrain from keeping the feet together, as this limits the power of the stroke.

BACK-FOOT — A batsman who is looking to play most of his shots off the back foot on pitches that are hard and have some pace and bounce. Most of his runs are cuts, pulls, hooks and drives off the back foot. There will be deflections down to fine leg and balls run down to third man. Bowlers need to bowl a fuller length to these batsmen to bring them more forward or onto the crease.

CREASE BOUND — A batsman who goes either back or forward but ends up on the crease, in a similar position to where he started. These batsmen are very susceptible to the lbw decision, being bowled and caught behind the wicket. Bowlers like bowling to these types of batsmen.

EXPLOSIVE — A batsman who will totally dominate the bowler and hit him out of the attack. He will hit boundaries and accept the challenge from a fast, intimidating bowler or a quality spin bowler.

DOUR — A batsman who is a defensive player and plays many dead bat shots at the ball.

ELEGANT/GRACEFUL — A batsman who has plenty of time to get into the right position to play his shots. He will have great eyesight and be light on his feet. He will time the ball well, often hitting the ball along the ground. When he hits the ball along the ground or in the air, he will hit it perfectly and sweetly, finding the gaps in the field, and often finding the boundary. He is technically very efficient.

NEAT AND COMPACT — Usually a smaller batsman who plays very correctly and within his limitations. He can play various types of innings but takes few risks. Usually scores most of his runs with pushes, drives and deflections.

GRITTY AND DETERMINED — A batsman who may not look pretty to watch but is still effective. He will play within his limitations and bat for long periods, collecting what runs he can.

PINCH HITTER — A batsman who is promoted in the order to get runs quickly. He will have a carefree approach, trying to hit sixes and fours because he has instructions to be positive and take some risks. His main job is to change the course of a match by forcing an early declaration or to win a match. He is usually promoted in the order to have a go against a spin bowler.

SLOGGER — A slang term for a batsman who has little or no technique and tries to hit nearly every ball to the boundary. Most of his shots are across the line of the ball and heaved away over mid-wicket and mid-on At times he will step away outside the leg stump, giving himself room to free his arms and hit the ball over mid-off or through the covers. There are plenty of miscues and the innings does not tend to last very long. A slogger is usually a bowler who likes to have a go when it is his turn to bat.

TAIL-ENDER — Usually a bowler who bats at number 9, 10 or 11. He does not score many runs but he can add support for a top-order batsman. Sometimes tail-enders are difficult to remove. They frustrate bowlers because they are technically deficient but somehow defend and hit the straight balls while playing at and missing the wider balls.

RABBIT — A batsman with little or no technique who is dismissed very quickly. He lacks concentration and is probably timid or scared, especially if a fast howler is in action.

FERRET — A batsman who comes in after a rabbit and has even less idea of how to bat. He carries a bat only because he has to. He should, however, always bear in mind that he can contribute to the score, sometimes very well, and add vital runs in the last wicket partnership.

NIGHT-WATCHMAN — A batsman, usually a tail-ender, who has a reasonable batting technique. He is given the responsibility of batting at the fall of a wicket, just before stumps, to protect a specialist batsman. His job is to bat out time and not be worried about scoring runs. Where possible, he should protect the other batsman and take as much strike as possible. If he does his job well, he will resume his innings the next day. Some night-watchmen love the opportunity to show everyone that they can bat. They sometimes make useful batting contributions to the team and frustrate the bowlers.

The orthodox grip. (Batsman shown without gloves to illustrate hand placement.)

The orthodox stance. This is a basic, comfortable stance. Many batsmen have their own variations.

DIFFERENT SHOTS PLAYED TO DEFEND A WICKET OR SCORE RUNS

Defensive shots are based around the batsman keeping his wicket intact and wearing the bowler down. They can be played off the front or the back foot. There will be times when a batsman will offer no shot at the ball because it is too wide for him to play at safely.

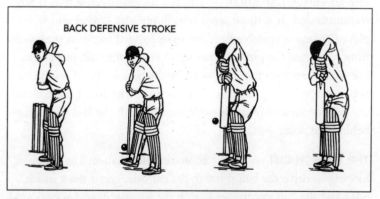

The attacking or scoring shots are the important ones. The following seven shots are scored off the front foot.

THE DRIVE THROUGH THE OFF SIDE OF THE FIELD — This could be a straight drive, a cover drive, or a square drive. There is also the on-drive on the leg side to mid-on or through mid-wicket.

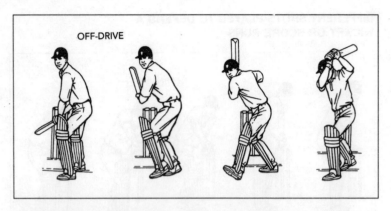

THE SWEEP or LAP SHOT — This is played to a ball usually pitched outside the line of the leg stump. The batsman places his front leg down the pitch and the knee of his back leg is on the pitch. The bat arcs or comes round the front leg and ball is played behind square on the leg side. The lap shot is a softer shot and paddled much finer to fine leg.

THE REVERSE LAP SHOT — This is a dangerous shot that is not recommended. It is more often seen in one-day cricket and is played against a spin bowler. The right-handed batsman pushes the front leg down the pitch, preparing to sweep the ball, but at the last second reverses the shot whereby the bottom hand on the bat becomes the leading hand and the batsman tries to hit the ball on the off side instead of the leg side, usually with the ball ending up behind the point area.

THE FRENCH CUT — This is an unintentional shot. The batsman, looking to drive the ball through the off side, gets a thick inside edge and the ball just misses hitting the leg stump and goes down to the fine leg position for a single or sometimes four runs.

THE PUSH — This is a shot where the ball is played into the gaps on both sides of the wicket. The batsman eases onto the front foot, waits for the ball to arrive and pushes the ball into an area where there are no fielders for a single or a couple of runs.

THE PULL SHOT

DEFLECTIONS — The ball that is turned down to fine leg or run down to third man. These are little deflections where the batsman uses the pace of the ball off the pitch and the angle of the bat to let the ball slide off and go very fine for easy runs.

THE PULL SHOT — Usually played off the front to a full toss.

The following shots are scored off the back foot.

THE CUT SHOT — The late cut and the square cut are played when the ball is pitched short and wide of the off stump. The square cut is hit with great power and usually goes behind point for four runs. The late cut is played much finer, usually off a spin bowler.

THE PULL SHOT — This shot, played to a short-pitched ball, is pulled onto the leg side behind square leg. The ball will go in the air for a short distance and usually produces four runs for the batsman.

THE HOOK SHOT — This full-blooded shot off a short-pitched ball, usually off a fast bowler, ends up scoring six or four. The ball, which stays in the air for a long distance, can be hit either in front of or behind square leg.

THE LEG GLANCE — The batsman eases onto the back foot, waits for the ball to arrive, then rolls the wrists over the ball, controlling it down to fine leg.

OPENING THE FACE OF THE BAT — The batsman waits for the ball to arrive, opens the face of the bat and, with the pace of the ball off the bat, the ball runs down to third man for a single. This is a dangerous shot to play off faster bowlers if two or three slips are in position. Batsmen can be caught out playing this shot. It is played with good effect in one-day matches when there are no slips.

THE FRENCH CUT — This is an unintentional shot played off the back foot the same as the front foot, even if the batsman is defending or attacking.

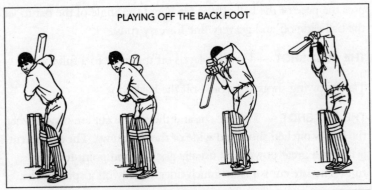

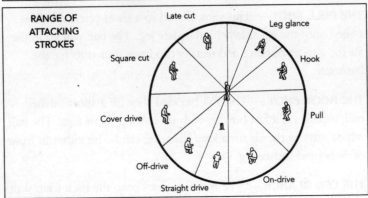

CHAPTER 7

Dismissals

A batsman can be dismissed in 10 different ways.

BOWLED *(Law 30)*

The batsman is out bowled when the ball delivered by the bowler breaks the wicket — i.e. causes one or both bails to fall — even though the ball has touched the batsman's bat, body or clothing.

CAUGHT *(Law 32)*

The batsman is out caught when the ball touches the bat — or the batsman's hand or glove holding the bat below the wrist — and is held by the fieldsman before the ball touches the ground.

HANDLED THE BALL *(Law 33)*

The batsman is out handled the ball if he picks up the ball or touches the ball with a hand not touching the bat, unless he does so with the permission of the fielding team.

HIT THE BALL TWICE *(Law 34)*

The batsman is out hit the ball twice if, after he has played the ball, or stopped it with his body, he strikes the ball again except for the purpose of protecting his wicket.

HIT WICKET *(Law 35)*

The batsman is out hit wicket if he breaks the wicket with any part of his bat, person or equipment, in the course of playing a shot at the ball or setting off for his first run.

LEG BEFORE WICKET *(Law 36)*

The batsman is out lbw when any part of his body (usually the pads) except the bat intercepts the ball which, in the opinion of the umpire, would have hit the wicket, provided that:

- The ball has pitched in line between the wickets from the bowler's end and the wickets at the batsman's end,
- the ball has pitched on the off side of the batsman's wicket and the point at which the ball has hit the batsman is in line with the wicket both ends,
- the ball has pitched outside the batsman's off stump and hit the batsman outside the line of the off stump and he has attempted to play no genuine shot at the ball.

(This law has been. designed to prevent the batsman deliberately playing no shot and padding up to the ball.)

The main considerations for the umpires when making an lbw decision are: the height of the ball when it strikes the batsman; whether the ball would have hit the wickets, and if there is an appeal made by the opposing side, usually the bowler and wicket-keeper. Any ball pitching outside the leg stump cannot be out lbw.

OBSTRUCTING THE FIELD *(Law 37)*

The batsman is out obstructing the field if he wilfully obstructs the opposition by word or by his actions, e.g. calling for a catch or impeding a fielder who may be attempting a catch or a run out.

RUN OUT *(Law 38)*

The batsman is run out if, when he is out of his ground, the wicket is broken by the opposing team. If the batsmen have crossed, the batsman running to the end where the wicket has been broken is out. If the batsmen have not crossed, the batsman running from the broken wicket is out.

STUMPED *(Law 39)*

The batsman is out stumped when, having received the ball from the bowler, he is out of his ground and the wicket-keeper, without any other fieldsman being involved, breaks the wicket with the ball in hand. If, however, the batsman is attempting a run, having played at and missed the ball, the batsman would then be adjudged run out and not stumped.

TIMED OUT *(Law 31)*

The batsman is timed out if he wilfully takes more than two minutes after the fall of the previous wicket to come to the crease. This very rarely happens, with the key word being wilfully. The law is based around preventing deliberate time wasting.

1. Out. The ball pitched outside the off stump but hit the pad on the line of the stumps and would have hit the wicket.
2. Out. Pitched on and would have hit.
3. Out. Pitched leg, moved towards off but would still have hit the stumps.
4. Out/Not out. Ball pitched outside the line and hit the pad, also outside the line. but would have hit the wicket. Not out if the striker made a genuine attempt to play the ball; out if he did not.
5. Not out. The ball pitched outside the line of the leg stump.

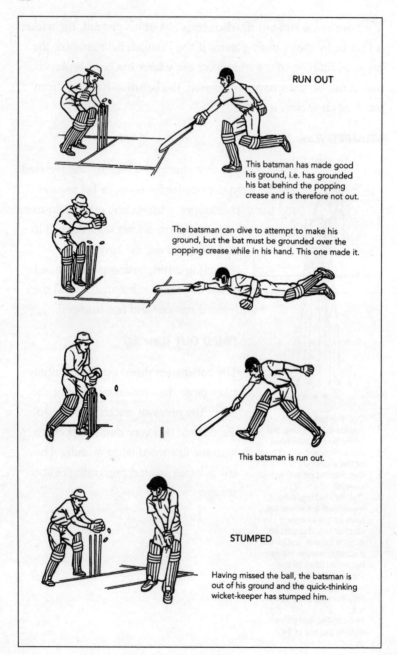

CHAPTER 8

Teamwork and Training

As a player, you have a responsibility to yourself, your team-mates, the selectors, the administrators and to the spectators. Believe in yourself and don't let yourself down. The following tips will be helpful.

- Always be on time for practice and matches.
- Practise your skills and correct your faults.
- Represent your team with pride.
- Do your job as well as you can.
- Respect your team-mates and the opposition and treat them as you would expect to be treated.
- Contribute at team meetings and planning sessions.
- Set your goals for the season. Write them down, record your performances and reassess when necessary.
- Play the game hard and to win, but play fairly.
- Play the game in the true spirit and within the laws of the game.
- Communicate with each other. Get to know your mates by learning something new about them.
- Check your playing gear to see that everything is in order and functional.
- Respect and accept the umpires' decisions, without question.
- Always congratulate the opposition at the end of the match.

- Be a gracious winner and a courteous loser.
- Always obey the team rules and disciplines set down by the management and/or players.
- Apply common sense in social situations. Ensure that alcohol consumption doesn't interfere with your playing performance the next day.
- Representative players at the highest level can be randomly tested for drugs. Always be aware of what substances in pharmaceutical medications are banned.
- Work hard for your team and team-mates because everyone will benefit. Work ethic is important as far as getting into good habits, disciplines and routines are concerned.
- Always cooperate with team officials and others associated with the game. Many people give their time freely to help the players succeed, enjoy and play the game.

PRE-SEASON TRAINING

ENDURANCE WORK — Distance running should be done for 40 minutes three times per week. Other options may include cycling or swimming sessions. Bowlers will need to do some sprinting work, for example, 10 30-metre sprints three times a week.

WEIGHT TRAINING — This is for strength, power, tone and muscle speed. It is important to seek advice from a professional and get an organised training programme that will suit your requirements. Whatever you do, don't go into a gymnasium and start lifting weights without proper supervision. Two sessions a week, depending on advice, will be beneficial.

CIRCUIT TRAINING IN GYMNASIUMS — This is a specially organised programme from a supervisor that will allow you to do various activities at pace. Two sessions a week, depending on advice, will be beneficial.

STRETCHING — Before you do any physical activity, you need to warm, up your muscles by stretching. This allows the body to become more flexible and mobile, reducing the risk of injury.

TECHNICAL TRAINING — All players need to work on their technique to make them more efficient and have a better chance of success. A good technique will produce better results, delay the onset of fatigue and tiredness and reduce the risk of injury. It will also allow for more repetitions of the skill before tiredness sets in. Pre-season bowling is usually confined to indoors so make sure you have proper footwear for the harder surfaces. Bowlers need to bowl in the nets before the season starts. This should be done at least twice a week. You should bowl no more than seven overs or 42 deliveries at one time. Bowlers should bowl at about 70-80 per cent and work on rhythm and being technically efficient — smooth run-up, take-off and elevation at delivery, body rotation, head position, ball release and follow through. Record the number of balls you bowl in a session. As the season gets closer, you may decide to increase the workload but break it down into two bowling spells. As soon as possible, practise bowling outdoors and get used to the different conditions.

Batsmen need to concentrate on their specifics in the nets. Recommended are 30-minute batting sessions concentrating on foot movement, head positioning, balance, poise, contact with the ball and bat follow through. It's important to bat against pace and spin bowlers. Some indoor facilities will have a bowling machine.

Wicket-keepers will need special training with a coach or teammate and, where possible, practice in the nets to spin bowlers.

MENTAL TRAINING — Start thinking about your goals or targets for the season. Write down what your expectations are and work out a plan of how you expect to achieve these goals. Be realistic about what you think you're capable of achieving. Review your goals at regular intervals.

NUTRITION AND DIET — This is becoming increasingly important. Studies prove that a proper diet is essential to enhance performance. The body needs to be supplemented with fibre, carbohydrates, protein and fluids because it is asked to expend a lot of energy through physical work. It is a good idea to talk to a dietician about your needs.

ASSESSMENTS — At the end of each session, or at specified times throughout the season, reassess where you're at with your training schedules, performances and targets. It is important to monitor your progress to see what areas need improvement.

As the season progresses, the general fitness and preparation outlined here need to be maintained but there will be a greater emphasis on the technical, mental and tactical aspects, with actual performances on the field determining how successful you are.

PRACTICE

- Have a plan of what you want to achieve during the session.
- Warm up before the session starts with a light jog and some stretching exercises.
- Do everything with a purpose and with intensity. Everything has to be about quality.
- Bowlers — Bowl in two separate spells. The first spell may be 40 minutes, then rest and come back for another 20-minute spell. Make sure there's an umpire in position to help you get close to the wickets and advise you if a no ball

has been bowled or if you're running on the pitch in the danger area. Concentrate on technique, rhythm, timing, consistency in line, length and variation. It is a good idea for fast bowlers to practise bowling with a new ball and an older ball to simulate match conditions. A bowler should always be looking to improve other aspects of the game by having batting and fielding drills.

- Batsmen — There should be at least one 20-30 minute batting session in the nets (this may not be possible at club practices). Try to keep your wicket intact during that session by not getting out. Where possible, keep the ball on the ground. Know where your off stump is and get used to letting balls go close to the stumps and playing at them. At some stage during the session, have some throw downs before or after the net session.

- Wicket-keepers — You need plenty of stretching, squats, sprints and catching practice. Try to catch 100 short, sharp catches off the bat from a team-mate. Where possible, practise your skills in a net while the batsmen are batting, especially to a spin bowler. Practise concentration on watching the ball, staying down as long as possible with your body weight on your toes. The head should be straight and still with the eyes level and the ball being caught at waist height. Make sure you also get some batting practice.

- Fielding — All players should be involved in a fielding session of approximately 20 minutes. During that period the emphasis should be on slip catching, cover catching and catching in the deep field. Ground fielding, including stopping the ball, picking up and throwing to the keeper, both underarm and overarm, should be practised.

- Games — The coach should try to make the practice sessions interesting and varied. Kicking and passing a rugby ball or a soccer ball is an enjoyable way to start and end a session, as well as being good exercise.

- Cool downs or warm downs — At the end of the session, all players should go for a light jog and do some final stretches to let the body unwind and relax.

- After a shower and a change of clothing, give yourself a rating on how well you performed, with the focus on the benefits achieved or areas that still need to be worked on.

Practice is about repetition, by doing it again and again until you perfect what you're doing. Then you keep doing it again and again until you're clinically efficient.

MATCH DAY ROUTINE

- Always be punctual. Arrive at the ground in plenty of time before the game is due to start: generally, this is at least 45 minutes before play starts. First-class and international players are usually at the ground 90 minutes before the game.

- Find your seat in the dressing room. You may like to sit in the same seat so you may have to ask another player to move. It can be a little upsetting if you have to move into another position.

- Check your gear and equipment.

- See the physiotherapist if necessary for any strapping that your body might need.

- Change into your tracksuit for pre-match practice.

- Walk onto the field of play, look at the general conditions, get the feel of the ground and have a look at the pitch. Bowlers will look for smooth run-ups, flat foot placements at delivery, the direction of the breeze whether there's any moisture in the pitch, the slope of the pitch or whether there's any grass or rough on the pitch to exploit. Batsmen will be looking for a dry, flat arid grassless pitch.

- Bowlers will select the ball they want to bowl with. Their choice will depend on colour, shape, feel and the size of the seam. A darker ball tends to swing more in the air.

- Warm up, including stretching and a light jog.

- Batsmen may have a net session with the bowlers having a light bowl. Special net bowlers are sometimes called into the session to rest the main bowlers. Bowlers will also have a bowl near the pitch from both ends to get used to the breeze and general conditions. This also allows the wicket-keeper to be involved.

- Fielding routines — catching, stopping the ball, pick-ups and throws to the keeper.

- Go back to the dressing room for a cup of tea, to relax and change into your playing gear. Make sure beforehand that you have the correct playing clothes.

- The captain comes back with the news of the toss (first day of the match only).

- More stretching. This is a good time to be thinking or focusing on your job role and expectations for the day.

➤ Drink fluids, preferably water. Make sure the twelfth man has your water bottle available for use during the day.

➤ If you're bowling first, talk to the captain about the end you want to bowl from and the field you want set.

➤ Enjoy the day.

SUMMARY

P   Practise and play with pride and passion.

L   Loyalty, trust and respect for your team mates,

A   Analyse and adapt to all types of conditions.

Y   'Yes, I can do it.' Have the confidence to go out there and perform to the best of your ability.

E   Enjoy the game and have high expectations.

R   Reliable performances and consistent results will make the game more enjoyable.

S   Stick to the simple basics of the game. Play within your limitations.

CHAPTER 9

The Role of the Captain

Captains are appointed by the selectors and generally approved by the local authority. They are usually easy, out-going people who have the respect of their team-mates. They're able to make decisions and are good communicators who can relate to the players.

It's often said that the best player doesn't necessarily make the best captain. Sometimes the best player is better left to playing the game and inspiring his or her team-mates with a brilliant individual or match-winning performance.
Captaincy is about leadership. In the words of Dwight D. Eisenhower, the 34th President of the United States, 'Leadership is the art of getting someone else to do something you want done because he wants to do it.'

THE QUALITIES REQUIRED OF A CAPTAIN

- ➤ Be a role model and lead by example. Set the standards as to dress, time, punctuality and the overall expectations of the team both on and off the field.

- ➤ Participate in all the activities that your team-mates do. This will help you gain respect through loyalty, trust and sincerity.

- Be a good organiser and planner by using time effectively and efficiently and asking the players to do the same.

- Be a positive decision-maker, by making decisions based on your experience and the advice given to you by coaches, managers and senior players. Decisions must be definite, consistent and in the best interests of the team. You should, however, never bow to pressure from those around you.

- Accept responsibility and be accountable for the decisions you make. There's no point in passing the buck and blaming others for failure or for making the wrong decision.

- Learn how to read the game — to adapt to certain match situations, to analyse batsmen to bring about their dismissal, to sort out the general strengths and weaknesses of the opposition and to assess how the pitch is playing and how the weather might influence the match.

- Play the game hard and to win, but above all play fair and within the laws and the true spirit of the game.

- Be positive in your approach. Make declarations in games that last two or more days and try to set up a possible result. This approach can be stimulating and refreshing for the players.

- Give the players a sense of purpose by allowing them responsibility. Give them the confidence to go out and show their talents so that they can enjoy and perhaps win the game. All the players need support and encouragement.

- Acknowledge the team if they have any successes. This will make the players feel good about themselves and ensure that their contributions have been valued and recognised.

➤ Have a thorough knowledge of the Laws of Cricket and gain an understanding of the local rules and conditions that will affect the match. Talk to the umpires about any special 'rules' that may apply to the match, e.g. start times, length of sessions, boundaries.

➤ Learn some aspects of history associated with the game by reading books and watching videos. Introducing cricket trivia to the players can be fun and create a good team spirit.

➤ Communicate clearly, with good diction, so that the players clearly understand the game plan, the tactics and the general expectations. These strategies are normally mentioned at team meetings. If there's a team coach or manager available, liaise with them.

➤ Have a good understanding and appreciation of the technical aspects of the game. There may be times when you need to offer a player some advice on a technical problem. Some teams have the luxury of a coach who can address these problems.

THE CAPTAIN'S TASKS

➤ Be involved with team warm-ups and practice sessions. There may be times when you'll need to appoint a vice-captain to coordinate and run the net practice sessions or a player to organise the warm-up or take the fielding sessions. Delegate responsibilities.

➤ In the absence of a team manager or coach, advise the team of the playing II. If there's a twelfth man, advise him before the meeting that he's been left out of the team, giving reasons for his omission. This will avoid any embarrassment and public disappointment for the player concerned.

- The toss. If you win the toss, decide whether to bat or bowl first depending on the pitch, weather conditions, your team's strengths, the opposition's weaknesses, the state of the competition and what needs to be done to win. a competition.

- Advise the team of the batting order. Put a note in the dressing room so that the players can see where they are required to bat. There may be times when you have to change the batting order, depending on the state of the match.

- If your team is fielding first, talk to your fast bowlers to see what end they want to bowl from and what sort of field they require. Always give the bowlers plenty of time to warm up and prepare. Be aware of the spells that a bowler can bowl before he becomes less effective. A fast bowler will normally be effective for five or six overs before he needs to be rested.

- In some forms of cricket, the batting side may be given the option of the use of a roller between innings. Decide whether you need the roller and, if so, whether the heavy or the light one. The heavy roller will bring any excess moisture to the surface and, if the pitch looks like breaking up, it will help to break it up further, which could be an advantage if the opposition has to bat last. The light roller will keep the pitch in a good, tidy batting condition for most of the match.

- Make the necessary bowling changes and ensure that the bowler has the right end to bowl from, depending on the wind, slope and condition of the pitch.

- Recalling the batsman is often a contentious issue and does not happen very often. Most players accept that the umpire is there to make the decision, whether he's right or wrong. Some captains, however, may feel strongly that if an opposition batsman has been victim of a bad decision, especially a catch at bat-pad, or a catch where the ball may not have carried, he may want to recall the batsman to continue his innings. Recalling the batsman is to be applauded because it reflects the true spirit of the game.

- The captain may be asked at times to make a declaration so that he can set a game for a possible result. The points to consider here are: Will the runs be scored too easily? What's the current run rate in the match? Is there enough time to bowl the opposition out? Will the weather play a part? What's the state of the pitch? Do we need to win the match? Can we afford to lose the match to allow the other team to win it and perhaps win the competition?

- At the conclusion of the match, the captain should thank the opposition players and congratulate them if they win. The other players should be encouraged to do the same. You would expect the same courtesy.

- In some cases the captain may be asked to say a few words on behalf of the team and to thank the opposition, the facilities, the groundsman, the umpires, the scorers and the people who have provided the lunches and the teas. Always be courteous and gracious.

- When, as captain, you're asked to speak to the media and make comments, always be constructive and positive. Praise the good aspects and suggest what areas may need to be worked on if there's room for improvement.

➤ In some cases the captain will be asked to write an umpire's report on the match. This usually happens in first-class and international matches. In other grades of cricket, there may be a card that needs to be filled in and sent to the newspapers so that they can publish the result of the match.

➤ Finally, the captain will need to enforce the discipline of the team. If the team has set the rules and a player breaks one of these, the problem must be dealt with quickly and efficiently, with the team knowing what action has been taken. If for example, a bowler is having problems with an umpire, step in and defuse the problem by reminding the player of responsibility to his team-mates and to the game in general. If a player is late for practice or late for the match or wears the wrong team attire, the team may impose a small fine. All rules and penalties need to be clearly defined before the season starts.

SUMMARY

C   Communicate with all the players so that they understand what's expected of the team.

A   Acknowledge successful team and individual performances.

P   Positive approaches to the game should be implemented.

T   Tactics should be planned and implemented.

A   Avoid cliques within the team.

I   Initiate full participation from the players at meetings, practices and on the field of play.

N   Never give up. Lead by example and compete in every match.

C   Calm players in agitated situations and play the game in its true spirit.

Y   You need to set the standards.

CHAPTER 10

Coaching

At any level of the game, the coach has a very responsible position. More often than not, at the highest level, the survival and the success of the coach is determined by the success of the team. The role of the coach will depend on the nature of the team. The coach of younger players will focus more on playing, having fun, developing skills and good habits. Plenty of adult guidance will be needed to establish and enforce disciplines.

International and first-class coaches will do similar things, but there'll be a greater emphasis on mental preparation, mental toughness and developing top fitness, consistent performances and achieving individual and team goals.

The most important aspect for the coach is getting the players to fulfil their potential.

GENERAL POINTS

➤ Attend a course and receive the necessary qualifications to be able to coach at the level you desire. In New Zealand cricket, there are three levels: Level one covers the basics relating to the technique required to play the game, level two is more advanced and level three takes in mental, physical, technical and tactical appreciation of the game, diet, motivation and running practice sessions efficiently and effectively. Some assignments through Massey University and from New Zealand Cricket are also necessary.

- Have a sound understanding of the game, especially the Laws of Cricket, and the local rules relating to playing conditions. Learn some of the history of the game.

- It's very helpful if you've played the game yourself. Playing at the highest possible level does not, however, mean that you'll be a successful coach. Any sort of playing experience should help you to relate to match situations and understand how the players may feel at certain times.

- Participating in training sessions with the players can gain immediate respect. If you're asking the players to do something, it's important that you can demonstrate the correct method. Set a good example through your own behaviour standards, appearance and knowledge of the sport.

- Analyse the game and make decisions that are in the best interests of the team and for the individuals. Adapt to situations quickly and decisively.

- Analyse player techniques and correct any faults but allow the players to show their skill or flair. Don't change or correct anything unless you can make some improvement for a player.

- Be a good communicator. Get the message across. Question the players and see what they think and understand how they feel. At team meetings encourage their full participation and thoughts.

- Be a motivator. Help to set team and individual goals and assist players to achieve those goals through thorough planning. Build the players up so that they have the confidence to perform in a range of conditions. Positive reinforcement goes a long way in gaining the players' respect. Never argue with the players or the officials. Use constructive criticism to encourage rather than degrade a person.

➤ Be involved in team selections. Congratulate those selected and offer feedback to those who were unsuccessful so that they are aware of the areas they must improve on to gain selection in the future.

➤ Help plan the tactics for the day's play, adapting to the prevailing match conditions. You need a game plan for the match that the team can follow, with tactics being reviewed at designated intervals.

➤ Be a person manager who can solve any problem that players may have. If there are any disputes, be fair but firm. Some of these may be personal so a fatherly or motherly approach may be necessary.

➤ Use all the resources that are available to you. If you lack the solution to a problem, call in someone who can assist. There will be times when a real expert will be of value; for example, if a bowler is having problems with his technique, perhaps a specialist bowling coach could help. You, as coach, will learn something too.

➤ The national coach and other top coaches may be involved in making some management decisions while on tour or playing in a tournament, e.g. the rooming list or delegating tasks to the players so that the tour runs smoothly. Some of the jobs will include looking after the scorebook, the flag, the team autograph sheets, practice balls, baggage, laundry, time, dress manager, team funds and the social committee that will organise fun activities for the team.

- Get to know the players outside of their normal cricketing surroundings, i.e. at golf, movies, etc. Remember, though, that there's a fine line between maintaining and losing the respect of the players. Don't get into a situation where players or parents may try to manipulate you and undermine or challenge your position.

- At team meetings invite the players to contribute and share their thoughts, opinions and emotions. It's important to get matters out in the open but in a closed environment. Anything discussed by the team should stay within the team. The environment should always be friendly and productive. Use these meetings to set the team goals.

- Always talk in terms of 'we' not 'I'. Everyone then has team ownership and feels part of the unit. Keep focused on the team goal (task cohesion) and keep the team spirit and team morale at a high level (social cohesion).

- Pair off rookies or new players with the more experienced or senior players so that the youngsters can learn from those who've 'been there and done that'. This certainly applies with rooming lists.

- Develop a team policy on awards. There will be times when an individual will win an award. Make it clear before the season or before the match what will happen to any awards, so that everyone understands beforehand. This will avoid disputes about what can be a delicate and touchy subject. As a general rule, any money goes into team funds but a player should be allowed to keep a trophy or prize.

- Develop a relationship with senior players in the team and ask them for a high level of commitment so that others will be encouraged to dig deep themselves.

- Develop a stable group with as few changes as possible. Try to keep the team settled with consistent selections that give everyone a fair go. The batting and bowling orders should be similar for each match unless special conditions apply. Scheduled practice times, apparel for the day and other routines should be consistent and everyone should be aware of them. This will create better team harmony.

- Be genuinely interested in the players as individuals, but avoid overplaying the more talented players in the team because the 'average' players need just as much, if not more, attention to help them perform.

- Develop a team respect for your opponents as well as for the officials and others associated with the game. Everyone has a job to do and should be respected and treated as being important.

- With the support of the local authority, encourage the team to wear the uniform with pride. Players can often lift their performances because they feel good representing their team.

AT TRAINING

- Use practice time efficiently and effectively so that the players get full value from the session. Everything done at practice needs to be of a high quality and be intensive. Players should feel that they've achieved something and that they've enjoyed the training.

➤ As a general rule, keep practice sessions to a maximum of two hours, with variation in activities. This will allow for full participation, and a high interest level, while reducing the likelihood of players becoming bored. Some sessions may need to be longer. If possible, ensure that players are aware of this before practice, especially in the case of junior and youth teams who may have parents picking them up at scheduled times.

➤ Give a pep talk on what needs to done and what your expectations are. Then ask for warm-ups, net session or open wicket practice, with a roster system stating when and where a player is involved. Demonstrate techniques if necessary. Some coaches may videotape the players so time may need to be set aside to analyse the video with the player. End each session with a quick appraisal of the practice session, so that the players know how they've performed.

➤ Keep records of how the players have performed and talk to them about their form and what needs to be done. It's essential to be fully conversant with the team and individual performances.

➤ Studying the form of the opposition players and teams will help you to plan tactics. You should also be aware of the pitch, ground and weather conditions. Basic homework about and understanding of what the team will experience can give you a decided advantage. Encourage the team to focus on any specifics so they learn to analyse the strengths and weaknesses for themselves. This will allow them to think, react and adapt. Players should try to perform within their limitations, sticking to the basics and keeping everything as simple as possible.

➤ Report to the various administrators/selectors on how the team and individuals have performed, making any recommendations that you feel are in everyone's best interests.

➤ Set the standards for the behaviour expected of the team, such as punctuality, dress and public appearances. Ask the players to represent the team with distinction and pride.

➤ Ensure that all the team gear and equipment and the practice facilities are available and up to standard.

SUMMARY

C   Control all situations and be calm.

O   Organisational stills should be implemented.

A   Attitudes should always be positive and constructive.

C   Communication with the players and the team must be at a high level.

H   High standards need to be achieved and maintained at all times.

1   Instruct and demonstrate the techniques correctly.

N   Natural player talent, flair and skill should be encouraged and expressed.

G   Goals for the team and for individuals should be set.

CHAPTER 11

Tips for Parents and Grandparents

Parents and grandparents play an important part in the development of young sportspeople.

➤ Encourage youngsters to play and enjoy a variety of sports, without pressurising them to be the best. Make sure children play to satisfy themselves and not to please parents or others in their peer groups. Don't force an unwilling child to play cricket.

➤ Be prepared by finding out where the game is being played, at least the night before, to avoid panic and stressful situations.

➤ Wherever possible, take youngsters to the ground and support their playing by encouraging them positively, and endorsing good sportsmanship and fair play. It can be a good idea for parents to roster travel to take youngsters to the ground.

➤ Be sympathetic in times of disappointments and congratulate them when they have achieved to make them feel special. Never ridicule children or yell when they make a mistake. Turn any mistakes into positives and work with them to correct the problem.

- Get to know the parents of other children on the team who may also be watching the game.

- Help with team social events. You could offer to host a barbecue, take the youngsters to McDonalds, a movie or to a test or a one-day international.

- Make sure the youngsters have some money to buy a drink or some food after or, if necessary, during the game. Alternatively, provide drinks and food for the player before they leave home.

- Sometimes a parent may be asked to umpire the game for a few overs. Familiarise yourself with the basic requirements of the Laws of Cricket and what the umpire is required to do. There's a lot more to umpiring than counting six balls in an over. (Refer to Chapter 15.)

- Encourage the youngsters to look after their gear and equipment. You may decide to buy them a bat, pads, gloves and other essentials. Make sure the gear fits and is comfortable. Seek advice from the sports shop.

- Make sure the youngsters are properly attired in whites so they look alike and feel part of the team. All too often, young players are seen in coloured tracksuits, sweaters, black shorts, etc. Also, unless they're practising, insist that the batting side watches the game and remains focused.

- In the backyard or at the park bowl to youngsters or let them bowl to you. Follow up with some fielding and catching practice.

- You may be asked to score. Familiarise yourself with Chapter 16.

➤ Get to know the person who's coaching your child. Find out if the coach is qualified in skill development and in injury prevention. Always be aware, however, that some coaches are volunteers who are doing their best. Try to work in with them. Praise the coach for a job well done. Be available to take over from the coach when necessary, e.g. when the coach is umpiring. Help reinforce the coach's philosophies to the youngsters.

➤ At some stage you may become a team selector. Obviously you'll want to pick the best team available to compete and win, but sometimes, at a very junior level, involvement, enjoyment and full participation are more important.

SUMMARY

P   Practise with your youngster.

A   Acknowledge areas of success.

R   Reinforce the Laws of Cricket and local rules that may apply.

E   Encourage fair play and team spirit.

N   Never criticise a player, coach or administrator in public.

T   Take youngsters to their games.

I   Instigate full participation in and enjoyment of the game.

N   Natural player talent, flair and skill should be encouraged and expressed.

G   Get to know other parents and the coach.

Chapter 12

Spectator Etiquette

To enjoy the game at the ground a spectator needs to be prepared.

- ➤ Buy a ticket well before the game starts so that you're assured of getting into the ground and sitting in a good seat. This certainly applies to one-day internationals when large crowds are expected.

- ➤ Buy a match programme. As well as interesting photos and player information, the programme will often contain a scorecard, career records and updates. This will help you to identify the players and give you a nice souvenir to mark the occasion. Some programmes become quite valuable, especially if they're autographed by the players.

- ➤ Take a soft cushion to sit on. If you are going to be at the ground for six or seven hours, some seats can become very hard. A chair is a good idea if you're on the embankment.

- ➤ Some spectators like to take a transistor radio to the ground so that they can listen to the radio commentators. A very few people may take a small hand-held television to watch the replays.

- ➤ Take binoculars so that you can get a close-up view of the action.

➤ Take a hat and sunglasses for protection from the sun. Wear sunscreen.

➤ Take extra clothing and a blanket for a cold day, and an umbrella if rain looks likely.

➤ Take something to read in case there's a stoppage in play.

➤ You may decide to take your own drink and food to the ground. Be aware that most grounds don't allow you to take alcohol into the ground but when inside you can purchase your requirements.

➤ If you're interested in collecting autographs, have your autograph book with you and a pen that works. Be polite rather than demanding when seeking an autograph.

➤ Some enthusiasts will take a scorebook to the match and record all the match details.

➤ If you're taking young children to a match, take a bat and a ball along for them to play with in the nets or on the back or outer ground. Make sure they're protected from the sun.

➤ Don't walk in front of the sight-screens at the bowler's end while an over is in progress. If there are no sight-screens at the ground, take care not to walk behind the bowler. This can cause unnecessary delays in play and puts the batsmen at an unfair disadvantage by upsetting their concentration.

SUMMARY

S   Support your team.

P   Prepare yourself for a day at the cricket.

E	Evaluate the state of play and read the game.
C	Clap, cheer and applaud the good aspects of the game, including the opposition's efforts.
T	Teach yourself more about cricket to make the game more interesting.
A	Avoid the sun at all times or make sure you're well protected.
T	Take your essentials to the ground for comfort and enjoyment.
O	Obey the local ground authority rules.
R	Relax and enjoy the game.
S	Secure a good seat.

CHAPTER 13

Commentators

Commentators have an important role to play because many people can't get to the grounds to watch a test, first-class or one-day match. Radio commentators need to paint pictures with the use of descriptive phrases so that listeners feel as though they are at the ground.

Television commentators have the pictures on the screen to tell the story, so they need to add information that is of interest for viewers. There are only two commentators on air at one time and after 20-30 minutes a new team will take over. There is a ball by ball commentator and there is a 'colour' commentator to contribute key thoughts on what *is* happening. The latter is usually a former player whose experience in the game adds interest. Some commentators can be very entertaining and very informative.

Commentators need to explain cricketing terms because there will be times when the game will sound very confusing and perhaps ambiguous.

RADIO COMMENTATORS

Commentators working in radio need at least some of the following qualities.

➤ Have a good command of the English language and get the point across with good diction.

➤ Allow the listener to 'see' the game through their eyes by setting the scene. They describe accurately what happens to every ball that is bowled and add details about the performances and the character of a player, giving player statistics. They mention the score as often as possible usually when a run is scored and at the end of an over because there are many listeners tuning in at different times during the game. They refer to some of the highlights during the day's play, reviewing the scoreboard, dismissals, fall of wickets and the bowling figures or analysis.

➤ Give the basic facts as concisely, quickly and clearly as possible using pauses.

➤ Relate to their fellow commentators and establish a rapport. A conversation that draws on the experience of the former player, who recalls and relates anecdotes, will interest listeners.

➤ Most radio commentators will be involved in player interviews and replay them on air at an appropriate time.

➤ Commentators should try not to talk over or interrupt each other. This sounds unprofessional and is bad manners. It can cause a commentator to lose his train of thought and can be distracting for listeners.

➤ It does not pay to criticise the umpires. It is better to explain why the umpire made a particular decision. An umpire gets only one chance to get the decision right whereas radio and television commentators may get to view the television replay three or four times from different angles before making a judgement.

➤ Always refer to the players by their surnames, although it is acceptable to use both the first name and the surname, e.g. Lara or Brian Lara.

➤ Be fair and as constructive as possible in analysing the game. There's no need to be controversial for the sake of it. Players will accept criticism if it's fair and constructive. Say what you think and believe in but offer some solutions to the problem.

TELEVISION COMMENTATORS

Most of the above also applies to television commentators, but there are some other aspects to be considered.

➤ They must always watch their television monitor or screen. This is the picture the viewers will see.

➤ Listen to the director or producer through their headsets because they can lead you into a situation that needs to be commented on.

➤ There is no need to describe the obvious because the viewer can see what is happening. Embellish the picture with constructive and interesting comment.

➤ Be careful not to describe something that is off screen but talk to the producer through the lazy mike or talkback microphone and get him or her to direct the cameras to that position. Also ask the producer for replays and be ready to talk about them.

➤ Always give the score at the end of the over before going into the commercial break.

➤ When on air, welcome viewers who may be watching from other parts of the world.

- Most television commentators are former players. They should develop a relationship that will be of interest to the viewers — a batsman commentator and a bowling commentator can produce a lively discussion.

- Television commentary is a team effort — some of the many different people involved are the director, producer, statistician, camera crew and those who get the pictures to air with the replays. Respect their roles.

TERMS USED BY COMMENTATORS

Some of the more common terminology used by all commentators.

DESCRIBING ASPECTS OF BATTING

- **That was a thick edge** — The batsman has mistimed the ball and the ball has hit the edge of the bat.

- **He was able to adjust** — The batsman was looking to play a certain shot at the ball, was deceived and was able to play another shot effectively.

- **He opened the face on that ball** — Instead of using the full face of the bat, the batsman angled the bat and allowed the ball to slide off it, usually behind point on the off side.

- **He's rolled his wrists over the ball** — The batsman waited for the ball to arrive then hit over the top of the ball, allowing it to be hit into the ground. This usually applies to a late cut or a sweep shot.

- **He's nicked the ball to the keeper** — The batsman has hit the ball with the outside edge of the bat and the ball has been caught by the wicket-keeper and the batsman is out.

- **He's top edged that sweep shot** — The batsman has tried to play the sweep shot, mistimed it and the ball has hit the edge of the bat and gone in the air.

- **He's miscued that shot** — This is a mistimed or a falsely induced shot by the batsman. The batsman has not hit very well and the ball usuall goes in the air.

- **The batsman's had a slash outside the off stump** — The batsman has played a forcing shot to a ball that pitched outside the off stump, missed it and the ball went through to the wicket-keeper.

- **He's tickled that one down the leg side** — The batsman has got enough bat on the ball, usually closing the face of the bat, and running the ball down to fine leg for runs.

- **He's hung the washing out to dry** — The batsman has played and missed at a ball that pitched outside the off stump and the ball has gone through to the wicket-keeper. The bat is waved at the ball as it goes past.

- **The batsman is batting on two legs** and **The batsman is batting on middle and leg** — This is the batsman's guard that he has asked for from the umpire. He will make a mark or block hole between the middle and leg stumps and he will place the toe of the bat on that mark when he takes strike.

- **The batsman is batting on middle stump** — The batsman's guard, block hole or mark is taken on the line of the middle stump.

- **He's been beaten all ends up** — The batsman has played and missed at a very good delivery from the bowler.

➢ **He's misread that delivery** — The batsman has failed to work out the type of delivery the bowler has bowled. This happens a lot when a leg-spinner is bowling because of the variations he has available, e.g. wrong 'un, flipper, leg-spinner or top-spinner.

➢ **The batsman is crease bound** — The batsman is attempting to play the ball from the batting crease. There is usually a lack of footwork because he is not sure whether he should play forward or back; the bowler has created indecision.

➢ **He's been trapped in front** — The ball has hit the batsman on the pads in front of the wickets and he is out lbw.

➢ **He's gone over the top** — The batsman has hit the ball over the top of the fieldsman, usually resulting in six or four runs.

➢ **He's got that one through the field** — The batsman has hit the ball along the ground between several fielders.

➢ **He's pierced the gap** — The batsman has hit the ball between two fielders.

➢ **He's too loose** — The batsman is playing very freely and is lacking correct technique. He's trying to score off nearly every ball that is bowled.

➢ **He's given his wicket away too easily** — The batsman has surrendered his wicket to the bowler easily and the bowler hasn't had to work enough to get him out.

➢ **That was a soft dismissal** — The batsman has given his wicket away far too easily by playing a poor or reckless shot, i.e. being easily caught, or running down the pitch, missing the ball and being stumped.

- **He's hit the ball over the top** — The batsman has hit the ball in the air over the fielder.

- **He's used the full face of the bat** — The batsman has hit the ball with the full blade of the bat.

- **He's defended well** — The batsman has played well to survive against a good bowler. He has taken no risks and frustrated the bowler by not getting out.

- **He's building an innings** — The batsman is spending plenty of time at the crease, taking no risks and accumulating runs with singles, twos and the odd boundary. He is looking to play sensibly and bat for as long as possible.

- **There's been a batting collapse** — The bowlers have dismissed a number of batsmen in short succession and cheaply.

- **He's scoring freely at the moment** — The batsman is on top of the bowlers and he is scoring runs easily and quickly without having to take risks.

- **There's been a change in the order** — The captain has rearranged the batting order depending on the state of the game, e.g. some quick runs may be required so a pinch hitter has been sent in to bat ahead of a recognised batsman.

- **He's scored a pair** — The batsman has been dismissed twice in the same match without scoring a run in either innings.

- **The ball's come off the thighpad** — The ball has hit the batsman's thighpad, usually resulting in a leg bye.

- **He's been bowled through the gate** — The batsman has been bowled by a ball that went between his bat and the pad because he failed to get his front foot to the pitch of the ball.

- **The batsman's been bowled around his legs** — The batsman has played and missed and the ball has gone behind his body and hit the wickets. This usually applies to a sweep shot off a spin bowler.

DESCRIBING BOWLING AND BOWLERS

- **The ball was seam up** — The seam of the ball, while travelling through the air, was perpendicular or upright.

- **The ball wobbled in the air** — The seam of the ball, while travelling through the air, was moving from side to side.

- **That ball floated with the arm** — Instead of trying to spin the ball, the spin bowler has bowled his arm ball. The ball has swung in the air or drifted away from the batsman from an off-spinner, or drifted in towards the batsman from a left-arm orthodox spinner. This is known as 'the arm ball'.

- **That ball leapt at the batsman** — The ball, usually off a good length, has bounced sharply off the pitch at the batsman, taking him by surprise. The pitch is usually in a deteriorating or poor condition for this to happen.

- **He is bowling his dibbly dobblers** — A part-time bowler who is barely bowling at medium pace. Some specialist bowlers will say that the ball is struggling to reach the other end.

- **That was a half tracker** — The bowler has landed the ball halfway down the pitch. This is a bad delivery and usually gets hit to the boundary.

➤ **He's beaten the batsman all ends up** — The batsman has played at and missed a well-bowled ball.

➤ **That was an unplayable delivery** — A ball that all bowlers want to bowl. The batsman may have done everything correctly but, all of a sudden, the ball has moved sharply in the air or off the pitch and deceived him.

➤ **That ball ran away from the right-hander** — The ball either moved in the air or off the pitch away from the right-handed batsman towards the slips, e.g. an outswinger or leg-cutter.

➤ **That one moved sharply** — The ball has moved quickly and sharply off the pitch or in the air, causing the batsman some problems.

➤ **That ball has flown off the edge of the bat** — The ball, bowled at pace, has bounced off the pitch, hurried onto the batsman, hitting the edge of the bat, and the ball has gone in the air. The batsman is sometimes caught out.

➤ **He's got some extra pace and bounce from that delivery** — The bowler has put some extra effort into the ball he has just bowled. The pitch has responded and helped him, often causing the batsman some problems with an unexpected result.

➤ **There's a bit of turn there** — The spin bowler has been able to get the ball to turn or deviate off the pitch.

➤ **There's a bit of spin there** — The spin bowler has got the ball to spin or deviate off the pitch.

- **That ball was going down leg** — The ball may have pitched on the stumps but was angling down the leg side and would have missed the leg stump. This is usually a reason why the umpire doesn't give the batsman out lbw.

- **That ball bit sharply** — The spin bowler has got the ball to turn, spin, deviate or bounce awkwardly off the pitch, causing the batsman problems.

- **That ball skidded through** — The ball hardly bounced, kept low and hurried onto the batsman.

- **That one kept low** — The ball 'died' or hardly bounced when it hit the pitch.

- **The bowler's on top** — The bowler is in control and dominating a batsman or the match. He's using the pitch and atmospheric conditions well and has good rhythm with the ball, which is consistently landing where he wants it to land.

- **A good, tight, accurate over** — The bowler has bowled a controlled over with few or no runs being scored by the batsman.

- **That was a good containing over** — The bowler has bowled a very good over with few or no runs being scored.

- **That was a poor delivery** — The bowler has bowled a bad ball and the batsman has scored easy runs from it, usually a boundary four or six. It could be a full toss, a long hop, a half volley or a ball that is wide of the off leg stump.

- **The bowler's hit the timbers** — The bowler has clean

bowled the batsman by hitting the wickets.

- **The bowler's rolling his arm over** — The bowler isn't putting a lot of effort into his bowling. He appears to be going through the motions. This also refers to a part-time bowler who comes on to bowl to try to break up a partnership or rest the main bowler.

DESCRIBING THE FIELDERS

- **The fieldsman's saving one** — The fielder is put in a position usually 15-20 metres from the bat to prevent the batsman from taking an easy single or run.

- **He's judged that well** — The fieldsman has taken a good catch.

- **He's giving chase** — The fieldsman is running after the ball.

- **He's dropped a dolly or a sitter** — The fieldsman has dropped an easy catch.

- **Caught in the slips** — The batsman has edged the ball off the bat and is out caught by one of the slips men.

- **Well stopped in the gully** — The fieldsman in the gully position has made a good save, preventing the batsman from scoring any runs.

- **The ball's gone through comfortably to first slip** — The batsman has edged the ball off the bat and the ball has carried through in the air to be caught by the fielder at first slip. The batsman is out.

MISCELLANEOUS TERMS

➤ **That's stumps** — After the last ball has been bowled, the umpire will say 'stumps' or 'time' meaning the end of the day's play.

➤ **Stumps are drawn** —When the umpires remove the wickets from the ground, it's usually the end of the day's play, or when rain comes the wickets are removed so the covers can be put on the pitch.

➤ **The ball has dislodged the bail** — The ball has hit the wickets and the bail has fallen to the ground, which will prompt an appeal from the fielding team to determine whether the batsman is out or not out.

➤ **At the fall of a wicket** — This is when a batsman has been dismissed. The team score at that time is recorded in the scorebook. For example, if at the fall of the first wicket the team score is 50, the opening partnership will have been 50 runs. If the fall of the second wicket is when the team score is 80, the second wicket partnership will be worth 30 runs.

➤ **The wicket's down** or **The wicket's broken** — The bail or bails have fallen off the top of the stumps or the wickets. If the batsman is out of his ground he can be out stumped or run out. If he misses the ball delivered by the bowler and the bail or bails are dislodged, then the batsman is out bowled.

➤ **Poor calling** — There are only three calls that should be used by a batsman: 'Yes' for a run, 'No', if there's no run, or 'Wait', if there's some indecision. After the wait call, there should be a yes or no call, depending on the situation. If a batsman is run out, it's usually through indecision and/or bad communication.

➤ **Bad light has stopped play** — The weather has deteriorated and it's got too dark so that the safety of the batsman is at risk, especially against a fast bowler. The umpires believe that the conditions are not fit for play and that one team is disadvantaged so they offer the batsmen the light. In most situations they will accept and play is suspended until the light improves.

➤ **The umpire's put his finger up** — The umpire has given the batsman out by raising his index finger.

➤ **He's been fired** — If in the opinion of a commentator, player or others associated with the game, the batsman has been a victim of a poor umpiring decision, the batsman is said to have been 'fired'. Some umpires who make quick and many decisions in a day, especially lbw decisions, are called 'trigger finger'.

SUMMARY

C   Communicate clearly with good diction to get the message across.

O   Opinions should be constructive.

M   Make sound and factual statements.

M   Mention the score as often as possible.

E   Entertain the listeners, viewers and the spectators.

N   Natural voice and manner will be more convincing than copying someone else's style.

T   Talk to the audience as though you're having a conversation with your co-commentator.

A   Analyse the game correctly.

T   Teach and educate the public more about the game, e.g. history, incidents, the laws, etc.

O   Observe every ball bowled and outline the tactics and the strategies used.

R   Resist making unfair criticism of the players and the umpires.

S   Summarise the highlights of the day's play at regular intervals.

CHAPTER 14

Umpires and Match Referees

Umpiring is a very demanding job that requires a high degree of fitness and concentration, and the ability to react under pressure and come up with the right decision.

Test, first-class and club umpires have to stand for at least six hours in the day concentrating on every ball that is bowled. They must count the balls in the over and signal to the scorers for byes, leg byes, wides, dead ball, sixes, fours and one short. They must watch the bowlers in case they run on the pitch and damage it, or bowl wides and/or no balls. They will be asked to hold the players' sweaters and to make decisions upon an appeal by the opposing side as to whether the batsman is out or not out.

The decisions umpires are asked to make must be judged on what they can see and hear. Although the fielders' reactions may be helpful when making decisions, umpires should not feel intimidated by appeals. As long as there is consistency in the decision-making process, the players will be more receptive and accept the decisions made.

THE QUALITIES REQUIRED OF UMPIRES

➤ Umpires need good eyesight. They should have their eyes

checked at regular intervals.

- Good hearing is essential. The ears should be checked at regular intervals.

- Umpires must be able to concentrate for long periods. Many top umpires use rigorous fitness programmes as they believe physical fitness greatly benefits their mental alertness. Lapses in concentration can result in mistakes and poor decision-making, which leads to player frustration and creates tense situations.

- They must attend an umpiring course and become qualified.

- Umpires must be familiar with and fully understand and appreciate the Laws of Cricket, and be aware of any changes that may occur.

- They must know the local association rules or playing conditions relating to the match, e.g. hours of play, start times, etc.

- Umpires must be firm and decisive and not be influenced or become emotionally involved with the game. If an umpire declines a decision such as an lbw and the bowler asks why it was not out, he or she should give a quick and simple explanation, e.g. 'The ball pitched outside the leg stump.'

- If an umpire makes a mistake, he or she should be strong, confident and brave enough to quickly alter the decision. This is in everyone's best interests and will gain immediate respect.

- Umpires must be relaxed and positive in their role. They must be themselves, not copying the style of anyone else, and they must enjoy what they are doing.

➤ Developing a rapport with the players and having a friendly chat between overs are part of the umpire's job. They should get to know the players and their capabilities. For example, if a batsman shuffles around the crease, they will be more vulnerable to an lbw decision than a batsman who looks to push well forward. They should give a bowler who is close to bowling no balls, or is running in the danger area, helpful advice. This helps the bowler make the necessary adjustments. A sound knowledge of the players' skills, personalities and characters can be helpful in avoiding volatile and perhaps explosive situations in a match and make decisions a little easier.

➤ Players like consistency, honesty, fairness and integrity. Umpires should therefore take care not to favour one team over the other, and should go about their job quietly and competently, without being noticed. Umpires are often criticised for being overly demonstrative and having too much influence on the game.

➤ The ability to read the game and understand what is happening for both teams makes umpires feel more involved in the match. They should ask themselves such questions as: Who holds the advantage? Who's playing well? Will the weather conditions change? Are the pitch conditions changing? What decisions am I likely to have to make? What do I need to know about a player's skill and ability?

UMPIRES' DUTIES

THE TASKS OF THE TWO UMPIRES TOGETHER

➤ Check to see that the pitch markings and alignments are correct and conform to the Laws of Cricket. The ground staff should have done this correctly, but they should be checked.

➤ Check the boundary markings so the boundary line is clearly defined.

➤ Put the stumps in the ground at each end of the pitch and make sure the height and the distance apart complies with the Laws of Cricket. Put the bails on top of the stumps.

➤ Before the toss, acquaint themselves with any special regulations. Some competitions have different rules.

➤ Discuss with both captains any conditions that will affect the conduct of the match, agree on one official clock or watch to be followed during play and ascertain the playing 11s of both teams.

➤ Check to see that the ball being used by both teams complies with the regulations.

➤ Before the game, check to see that the ground has adequate covers in case of rain.

➤ Find out who has won the toss.

➤ Find out from which end the first over of the match will be bowled.

➤ Give the teams at least five minutes' notice before play is due to start.

- Walk out together onto the field of play five minutes before play is due to begin.

- Ensure the field is cleared of spectators, nets, playing equipment and any other obstructions.

- Check to see that no more than 11 players are on the field of play.

- When it rains, ensure that the covers are put on the pitch as soon as possible.

- Both umpires are responsible and are sole judges of unfair play. They must enforce the Laws of Cricket. The umpires are responsible for decisions relating to the fitness of the playing conditions, time wasting, excessive and persistent short-pitched bowling, player abuse, dissent, sledging and slow over rates. They should take the appropriate action with warnings, etc.

- All disputes are determined by the umpires. If they disagree, then the current state of play will continue.

- Before the start of play and between innings allow for the pitch to be rolled for seven minutes.

- Where necessary make a report to the local authority if there has been a breach in the Code of Conduct.

- Check to see that the scorebook has the correct score.

- In a two-innings match, change ends for the start of the second innings.

- One of the umpires will be responsible for the safe keeping of the match ball during the intervals or breaks in play.

- Check the match ball at regular intervals to ensure that it has not been tampered with.
- At intervals, record which batsman will take strike at the resumption of play. Make sure that a bowler does not bowl two consecutive overs when play resumes.

THE TASKS OF THE UMPIRE AT THE BOWLER'S END

- Give the bowler his marker.
- Give the batsman his guard or block hole.
- Check to see that the sight-screens are in the correct position for the batsman.
- Signal to the scorers that play is about to begin.
- Call 'Play* for the game to start.
- Count six fair deliveries in one over and at the end of the over call 'Over' and move into the square leg umpiring position.
- Call 'Time' on the cessation of play before the intervals, interruption of play, or at the end of the day's play.
- Call 'Dead ball' when applicable.
- Signal no ball, bye, leg bye, one short, wide, boundary four or six to the scorers and ensure the scorers acknowledge the signals.
- Outs include lbw, caught, handled the ball, hit wicket, hit the ball twice, run out, obstruction, timed out and bowled.
- In televised international matches, the umpire can use the

services of the third umpire to help make a decision. The umpire makes a signal by drawing an imaginary square and the third umpire uses the video replay to determine the correct decision. These decisions usually relate to a batsman being caught out, run out, slumped, whether a four or six has been scored or whether a player has come in contact with the ball and the boundary line.

➤ Give consent for a fielder to leave the field of play. Take note of the time when he leaves and when he returns.

➤ Make sure the close-in fielders do not encroach on the pitch when the bowler is running in to bowl.

➤ Call and signal a short run if the batsman fails to make his ground when attempting more than one run.

THE TASKS OF THE UMPIRE AT SQUARE LEG

➤ Count the number of balls in the over and support the other umpire by signalling that the over has been completed.

➤ Call and signal a short run if the batsman fails to make his ground when attempting more than one run.

➤ Check the fairness of the delivery and making sure the ball is bowled and not thrown.

➤ On appeal from the fielding team make a decision whether a batsman is out — slumped or run out at his end. He may be asked to assist his colleague to adjudicate on other possible dismissals — hit wicket, handled ball, hit the ball twice, bowled, caught, timed out, obstruction.

➤ Call 'Dead ball' when applicable.

- Check to see that there are no more than two fieldsmen positioned behind square on the leg side.

- Call and signal 'no balls' that are within his jurisdiction, e.g. a bowler throwing the ball at delivery, more than two men behind square on the leg side. In one-day matches signal to the umpire at the bowler's end when a fall toss delivery is above the waist or when a short-pitched ball is above the chest.

- Watch the wicket-keeper to make sure that no part of his body or the gloves are in front of the wickets when the ball is being bowled.

- Watch for all forms of unfair play and adjudicate when necessary.

- After six balls have been bowled, move into the umpire's position at the bowler's end.

WHAT AN UMPIRE MAY CARRY

- A ball counter to count the balls in an over. The counter may be six matches, pebbles or a specially designed counter.

- Pencil and pad to write down any notes during the day's play or to record the number of overs bowled by a bowler in a one-day match. Sometimes a special card is provided to record the number of overs.

- A reliable watch by which the playing time is judged.

- Sticking plaster in case a player receives a cut or graze while in the field.

- Scissors or a pocket knife to cut a loose thread off the ball or to clean dirt off a player's boot studs.

- Tape measure to check that the pitch dimensions are correct.

- A ball gauge. There may be times when a ball goes out of shape. If the ball fits through this gauge then generally play will continue with the same ball.

- The umpire may carry a spare ball, but a selection of spare balls are available in the umpires' room.

- A spare set of bails should be available in case there is a breakage. Sometimes heavier bails are available in case there is a strong wind.

- Chewing gum.

- Lip cream and sunscreen.

- Some umpires may carry an insect repellent in some conditions.

- A piece of towelling or a rag in case a wet ball needs to be dried.

- A copy of the Laws of Cricket to refer to if necessary.

- A copy of the local authority rule book to refer to special playing conditions which may apply.

- A bowling marker, usually a plastic or metal disc, which the bowler uses to mark the commencement of his run-up. An umpire should wear a white coat or jacket. He should wear a hat, and in some cases sunglasses are sensible and acceptable. In lower grades of cricket it is important that player umpires wear something different from their playing whites so they are not confused with the fielders.

SUMMARY

U   Uphold the Laws of Cricket and the local rules applying to that match.

M   Make the correct decisions based on what you see and hear.

F   Prepare yourself for the match physically and mentally, and fulfil your duties.

I   Insist on fair play from both teams.

R   Rapport with the players will gain respect.

I   Identify where the scorers are positioned, signal to them and get their response.

N   Neutralise possible volatile situations.

G   Give the batsman his guard.

THE MATCH REFEREE AND HIS DUTIES

The match referee is used only at international matches. He is appointed by the ICC and his duties include the following:

- Represent the ICC and ensure that Law 42 is properly adhered to as far as unfair play and the Code of Conduct are concerned.

- Be on the ground at all times while a match is in progress, including being out in the middle of the pitch to supervise the toss between the two captains on the first morning of the match.

- Ensure that the spirit of the game is maintained both on and off the field.
- Liaise with the host nation's administrators and local ground authorities.
- Liaise with the umpires without interfering with their traditional role.
- Where there is a dispute or misunderstanding, interpret the Laws of Cricket and local rules.
- Some of the key issues the referee needs to monitor are: the over rates, persistent short-pitched bowling, failure to comply with the ICC regulations relating to advertising on players' clothes and player equipment, player dissent, verbal abuse or sledging, not accepting the umpire's decision, and any other activity that brings the game into disrepute.

In a test match, a minimum of 90 overs must be bowled in a day. In a one-day international 50 overs must be completed within three and a half hours. If there are breaches in any of the above the referee can take action.

(i) To impose penalties on any breach of the Code of Conduct. These penalties can be a fine, suspension or a reprimand.

(ii) File a report to the ICC secretary on any breach, covering the player's name, date of the incident, the venue, the incident and the appropriate action taken.

Any Code of Conduct breach can be reported to the match referee by an umpire, team manager, chief executive officer or his nominee member of the board.

THE INTERNATIONAL CODE OF CONDUCT

The International Code of Conduct includes the following:

- The captains are responsible at all times for ensuring that play is conducted within the spirit of the game as well as within the Laws of Cricket.

- Players and team officials shall not at any time engage in conduct unbecoming to an international player or team official, which could bring them or the game into disrepute.

- Players and team officials must at all times accept the umpire's decision and must not show dissent at the umpire's decision.

- Players and team officials shall not intimidate, assault or attempt to intimidate or assault an umpire, another player or a spectator.

- Players and team officials shall not use crude or abusive language (known as sledging) nor make offensive gestures.

- Players and team officials shall not use or in any way be concerned in the use or distribution of illegal drugs.

- Players and team officials shall not disclose or comment upon any alleged breach of the code, or upon any hearing, or report a decision arising from such a breach.

- Players and team officials shall not make any public announcement or media comment which is detrimental either to the game in general, or to a particular tour in which they are involved, or about any tour between other countries which is taking place, or to relations between the boards of the competing teams.

(ICC Regulations, October 1991)

THE UMPIRE'S SIGNALS

Out —
a raised index finger above the head.

Leg bye —
a hand touching a raised leg.

Bye —
an open hand raised above the head.

Dead ball —
call 'Dead ball' with arms crossing back and forth at knee level.

Television replay — the on-field umpire signals to the third umpire by making the shape of a television screen with his hands.

Altering a decision — arms crossed in front with fingers on shoulders. The umpire must wait for the scorers' acknowledgment and then give the amended signal.

Wide —
call 'Wide' with both arms extended horizontally.

No ball —
call 'No ball' with one arm extended horizontally.

Boundary four —
an arm waved horizontally from side.

Short run —
call 'Short run' with an arm bent to touch the shoulder.

Boundary six —
both arms raised vertically.

CHAPTER 15

How the Game is Scored

All players and coaches should have a basic understanding of how to score a cricket match in the scorebook. There will be times when a parent may be asked to score for a few overs. Spectators often take a scorebook to the park and enter all the march details during a representative or international match. An example of a scoresheet is given on page 115.

THE SCOREBOOK

The scorebook is broken into four basic sections:

1. Batting scores and dismissals, including the extras (wides, no balls, leg byes and byes).

2. The fall of wickets.

3. The total runs scored.

4. The bowling analysis.

Every ball bowled during the match has to be recorded accurately. This takes a great deal of concentration. After a ball has been bowled and runs are scored, the batting, bowling and total sections need to be filled in. If no runs are scored, only the bowling area is used to record the dot ball.

BATTING

- The batting order is listed from number one to number 11.

- Runs scored by the batsman are credited to his name. They have to be hit by the bat or from below the wrist of the hand holding the bat.

- When a batsman has been dismissed, describe how out in the batting column and record the bowler's name. If a batsman is run out, the bowler's name is not mentioned.

- When a batsman is dismissed, his innings is closed off and you draw a line after the last runs he scored, e.g. //.

- Extras are recorded in the area provided. Wait for the umpire's signal and acknowledge it.

- If a batsman scores runs from a no ball, those rims are credited to the batsman's score,

- All other extras are recorded in the area provided, e.g. byes, leg byes, wides.

FALL OF WICKETS

At the fall of a wicket, enter the team total in the box provided when the wicket fell. Ten boxes are provided for each of the wickets that may fall during an innings.

TOTAL RUNS

When a run is scored cross the run or runs off the total runs column. This accumulated total is the final score and must balance with the batting scores, including all the extras, and the bowling figures, which will also include leg byes and byes.

BOWLING

➤ List the name of the bowler in the bowler's column.

➤ After each ball has been bowled, enter what happened in the squares provided. Each square signifies one over in which six balls (more if there are wides and no balls) must be bowled.

➤ The number of runs scored from that over are added to the accumulated runs at the end of the previous over. These figures are put in the small box in the square. In some scorebooks it may be necessary to draw your own box to record the accumulated bowling figures.

➤ Wides and no balls count against the bowler and are recorded in the squares and added to the accumulated bowling figures at the end of the over.

AN EXAMPLE OF A SCOREBOARD

A basic scoreboard that shows the home team having scored 54 for 1 in reply to the visitors' score of 179. Batsman number 1 has scored 30; number 3 has scored 2. The last man out scored 18 runs and the last wicket fell at 45 runs. The innings is in the 12th over. The figures can be removed from their pegs or operate from within on a simple 'belt' system.

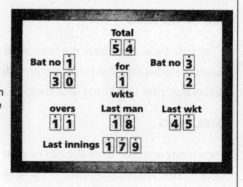

HOME CLUB New Zealand **CRICKET CLUB V** Australia **C. CLUB**
INNINGS OF New Zealand **PLAYED AT** Eden Park **ON** 28 March **ON 19** 93

#	BATSMEN	RUNS SCORED	TOTAL	HOW OUT	BOWLER	TOTAL
1	B.J. Latham	1.4.1.4.4.3.1.1.3	22	C.M. Waugh	Hughes	22
2	M.J. Greatbatch	1.1.1.1.2.4.2.1.1.4.4.1.1.1.1.1.1.1.4.2.1.1.1.1.1.4.1.1.6.1.1.1	68	C. Border	S. Waugh	68
3	A.H. Jones	1.1	2	St. Healy	May	2
4	M.D. Crowe	1.1.1.4.2.1.1.1	11	LBW	May	11
5	K.R. Rutherford	1.2.1.1.1	6		RUN OUT	6
6	T.E. Blain	1.1.1.1.2	8		RUN OUT	8
7	J.W. Wilson	1.2.4.1.4.1.1.1.1	21	C. Border	Dodemaide	21
8	D.N. Patel	1.1.6	8	C.M. Waugh	S. Waugh	8
9	C.J. Larsen	1.1.2.1.1.2.2.1.1.6.1.1.1.1.4.2.2.2	33		NOT OUT	33
10	C. Pringle	1.2.2.1.1.1.4.1.1.4.1.1.2	22		NOT OUT	22
11	D.K. Morrison					

EXTRAS 28
TOTAL 229
FOR 8 WKTS.

RUNS AT THE FALL OF EACH WICKET AND No. OF NOT OUT BATSMAN

1	2	3	4	5	6	7	8	9	10
50	61	91	114	130	139	166	175		
1	3	4	5	2	6	8	7		

BOWLING ANALYSIS

BOWLERS	OVERS	MAIDENS	RUNS	WKTS
1 M.G. Hughes	10	0	46	1
2 A.I.C. Dodemaide	10	1	39	1
3 P.R. Reiffel	10	0	49	0
4 S.A. May	10	0	40	2
5 S.R. Waugh	8	1	27	2
6 M.E. Waugh	2	0	9	0

UMPIRES 1 B.L. Aldridge 2 D.B. Cowie   **SCORERS** 1 S.J. Montgomery 2 A.D.K. Boswell

SYMBOLS USED IN THE BOWLING SECTION

- •   Dot ball — no runs scored off the bowler.
- 1-6   One up to six runs scored off the bowler.
- w   When a bowler captures a wicket.
- M   A maiden over bowled (no score from six balls).
- *W*   A wicket maiden bowled.
- +   A wide ball bowled by the bowler.
- Ll   Signifies one leg bye; L4 is four leg byes, etc.
- Bl   Signifies one bye; B4 is four byes, etc.
- R   A batsman has been run out.
- (2)   Two within a circle signifies a no ball and the batsman has scored two runs. Credit goes to the batsman.
- (•)   A dot within a circle signifies a no ball and no runs scored off the bat. (One no ball is entered in the extras section.)

SUMMARY

- S   Sharpen your pencil, have a rubber or pen available.
- C   Confirm and acknowledge the umpire's signals.
- O   Observe every ball that is bowled.
- R   Record every ball that is bowled in the scorebook.
- I   Identify your scoring position for the umpires.
- N   Neatness and accuracy is required at all times.
- G   Gather all the information and check that the batting, bowling and extras tally correctly.

CHAPTER 16

Personal and Team Equipment

PERSONAL EQUIPMENT

Many players prefer to have their own personal equipment. It is always an advantage to play with equipment that you are comfortable with and that is well looked after.

- Cricket carry bag. This is often a nylon bag that carries all the gear or has an external zipped pouch to carry a bat. Most international and first-class players use cricket cases or 'coffins'.
- A personally selected cricket bat and bat cover. Some players also have a spare bat.
- One, maybe two, pairs of batting gloves.
- One pair of pads.
- A wicket-keeper may have his own pair of wicket-keeping pads, gloves and inner gloves.
- Thighpad and inner thighpad.
- At least one practice ball.
- Arm guard.

- Chest protector.

- Abdominal protector or box and an athletic support or jock strap for a slip-in box.

- Cap and/or sunhat and/or sunglasses.

- Helmet.

- Playing whites that include two shirts, a pair of fielding trousers, a pair of batting trousers, two pairs of woollen socks, a sleeveless and long- sleeved sweater and a vest or singlet.

- Boots. A pair of bowling boots if you are a bowler and a pair of lighter boots for batting.

- Other miscellaneous items may include spare studs, a sprig tightener, a spare pair of laces, sandpaper to clean the bat, bat oil, a spare rubber grip for the bat to replace a damaged one, a bat grip cone tool to put on a spare grip, a bat hammer to break in a new bat, a pair of wrist bands, a headband, a drag plate to protect the toe of a bowler's boot.

- A private first aid kit would include Band-Aids, bandages, sunscreen, lip cream, massage cream, scissors, a knife, cotton wool, glue, a screwdriver, sponge rubber, needle and cotton, chewing gum, aspirin, vaseline and tinea powder to prevent blisters and foot skin rash, and some antiseptic cream for cuts and grazes.

- Most bowlers will have a pair of inner soles in their boots or orthotics (used for those bowlers who have high arches and need support) to help protect and cushion the feet. A spare pair is advisable. Some players may need ankle supports, knee bandages and other items to protect injuries.

- Money to buy a drink and some food, or take your own to

the match. It is important to take something to drink to avoid dehydration.

SELECTING A BAT SIZE

Ages 8-11	Batsman up to 145 centimetres in height	Size 4
	Batsman above 145 centimetres	Size 5
Ages 11-14	Batsman up to 158 centimetres in height	Size 5
	Batsman above 158 centimetres	Size 6
Ages 14-16	Batsman up to 165 centimetres	Size 6
	Batsman above 165 centimetres	Harrow
Over 16	Batsman up to 170 centimetres in height	Harrow

A full-sized bat can have a short or a long handle. Make sure you feel comfortable with the bat you've selected. Check the following points:

➤ It is better to select a lighter bat than one that is too heavy.

➤ Feel the pick up and the grip of the bat to see that it is balanced to your liking.

➤ Look at the grain down the middle of the bat. Ensure that it is not too wide or too narrow and that there are no knots in the wood.

➤ Some bats have a poly-coated or plastic film coating over the blade of the bat (it must not exceed 1/16 of an inch in thickness). This gives the bat a slightly longer life and makes it easier to keep clean.

➤ A bat that has no protective coating will need to be maintained by using sandpaper to keep it clean. Also apply a light coating of bat or linseed oil to the blade two or three times during the season to keep it in good condition.

➤ It is wise to select a well-known brand. Top grade bats are made of English willow, cheaper ones from Kashmir willow.

➤ The bat must not exceed 38 inches (96.5 centimetres) in height and at its widest part should not exceed 4 1/4 inches (10.8 centimetres). On average the weight will vary from 2 lb 6 oz to 3 lb (1.08 to 1.36 kg).

TEAM EQUIPMENT

Coaches, captains and/or players should make sure that the basic team gear requirements are available for each match. The following list shows the basic essentials, followed by optional extras, depending on the grade and type of cricket played and what the coach may require.

THE BASICS

➤ Canvas gear bag with side straps and straps at each end of the bag, to make carrying by two players easier.

➤ Three bats, preferably medium weight and short handled.

➤ Four pairs of pads (three pairs for right-handed batsmen, and one pair for a left-handed batsman).

➤ Four pairs of batting gloves (three pairs for right-handed batsmen and one pair for a left-handed batsman).

➤ Three abdominal protectors or boxes.

➤ Three thighpads that can be used by either a right- or a left-handed batsman.

- One pair of wicket-keeping gloves and a pair of inner gloves.
- One set of six stumps complete with four bails.
- A match ball and approximately six practice balls.
- A scorebook with two pencils and a rubber.
- Two umpire's ball counters to count the balls bowled in the over (one for each umpire).
- Medical kit with such basics as Band-Aids, sunscreen, scissors, a knife, bandages, antiseptic cream, massage cream, aspirin and cotton wool.
- Portable scoreboard.

Before the season starts, all the equipment must be checked to see what needs to be repaired, replaced and cleaned.

EXTRAS

Some coaches may have the following items available to help with training drills.

- A rugby or soccer ball for general running around before and after practice.
- A tennis racquet and approximately three tennis balls for close catching and reflex skills.
- A baseball glove for catching cricket balls to protect the hands at practice in some of the fielding drills.
- A super-short or cut-down cricket bat for close catching routines including slip and bat-pad catches.

SUMMARY

E   Essential and basic equipment should always be in your kit bag.

Q   Quality gear should be used.

U   Untidy kit bags can lead to damaged and missing items.

I   Inspect your gear regularly for items that may need fixing, replacing or cleaning.

P   Personally select your equipment to suit your requirements.

M   Medical kits are handy additions to kit bags.

E   Evaluate the performance of your gear — is it doing the job for you?

N   Never leave your gear unattended in a car and ensure the dressing room is secure.

T   Take care of your gear — it is the tools of your trade.

CHAPTER 17

Administrations and Trophies

WORLD GOVERNING BODIES

ICC — International Cricket Council
Founded as the Imperial Cricket Conference on 15 June 1909, it was renamed the International Cricket Council on 15 July 1965. This world body governs the game of cricket. Full membership comprises the test-playing nations: Australia, Bangladesh, England, India, New Zealand, Pakistan, South Africa, Sri Lanka, the West Indies and Zimbabwe. Other members include Argentina, Bermuda, Canada, Denmark, East and Central Africa, Fiji, Gibraltar, Hong Kong, Ireland, Israel, Italy, Kenya, Malaysia, Namibia, Nepal, the Netherlands, Papua New Guinea, Scotland, Singapore, the United Arab Emirates, the United States and West Africa. The headquarters are The Clock Tower, Lord's Cricket Ground, London NW8 8QZ.

MCC — Marylebone Cricket Club
This is a private cricket club with its headquarters based at Lord's Cricket Ground (named after Thomas Lord in 1787) in London. The MCC established the Laws of Cricket. The patron of the club is Her Majesty the Queen. Membership was restricted to men only for 211 years, until 1998 when the members decided to allow

women to join them. The famous pavilion hosts the Ashes urn in the Long Room. There are many other historical pieces of memorabilia on show including bats, balls and prints.

The MCC has led the way in promoting and developing the game through coaching young players, playing against schools, touring and promoting the right spirit of the game.

ECB — England and Wales Cricket Board
The ECB is responsible for the administration of all cricket in England and Wales, whether it is professional or recreational. All the first-class and minor counties are represented. It used to be known as the TCCB (Test and County Cricket Board).
The ECB is based at Lord's Cricket Ground, London NW8 8QZ.

NZC INC. — New Zealand Cricket Incorporated
Used to be known as the New Zealand Cricket Council (NZCC)
Box 958, Christchurch, New Zealand.

ACB — Australian Cricket Board
90 Jolimont St, Jolimont, Melbourne, Victoria 3002, Australia.

UCBSA — United Cricket Board of South Africa
Box 55009, Northlands 2116, Transvaal, South Africa.

BCCI — The Board of Control for Cricket in India
Sanmitra, Anandpura, Baroda 390001, India.

PCB — Pakistan Cricket Board
Gaddafi Stadium, Ferozepur Road, Lahore, Pakistan.

BCCSL — Board of Control for Cricket in Sri Lanka
58 Campbell Place, Colombo 10, Sri Lanka.

WICB — West Indies Cricket Board
Box 616 W, Woods Centre, St Johns, Antigua.

ZBU — Zimbabwe Cricket Union

Box 2739 Harare, Zimbabwe.

BCB — Bangladesh Cricket Board
Bangabandhu National Stadium, Dhaka, Bangladesh.

NEW ZEALAND CRICKET ASSOCIATIONS

ACA Auckland Cricket Association
Box 56-906, Auckland, phone (09) 8154855, fax (09) 8464464.

CCA Canterbury Cricket Association
Box 789, Christchurch, phone (03) 3663003, fax (03) 3653073.

CDCA Central Districts Cricket Association
Box 309, Napier, phone (06) 8355470, fax (06) 8350543.

NDCA Northern Districts Cricket Association
Box 1347, Hamilton, phone (07) 8393783, fax (07) 8395542.

OCA Otago Cricket Association
Box 1419, Dunedin, phone (03) 4554056, fax (03) 4554250.

WCA Wellington Cricket Association
Box 578, Wellington, phone (04) 3843171, fax (04) 3843498.

TROPHIES PLAYED FOR

AUSTRALIA
- Ansett Australia Test Series: between Australia and a touring team.
- Carlton and United Series: one-day international matches between Australia and a touring team. Originally known as WSC, World Series Cricket.
- Pura Milk Cup (formerly known as the Sheffield Shield):

four-day first-class matches between the states of New South Wales, Queensland, South Australia, Victoria, Tasmania and Western Australia.
- Mercantile Mutual Assurance Cup: 50-over one-day competition between the six state teams.

ENGLAND
- The Ashes: the test match series contested between England and Australia,
- Cornhill Insurance Test Series: test matches against visiting teams.
- Texaco Trophy: one-day series against visiting international teams.
- PPP Healthcare County Championship: contested by all 18 first-class county teams. (Two divisions.)
- Norwich Union National Cricket League: 45-over league competition contested by all the first-class county teams. (Two divisions.)
- Benson and Hedges 50-over One-Day Competition: contested by all the first-class county teams and Scotland. Regional qualifying rounds, with the two top teams in each group qualifying for the quarter finals; the final is held at Lord's.
- NatWest 50-over One-Day Competition: contested by all the first-class county teams and the minor county teams on a knockout basis; the final is held at Lord's.

INDIA
- Ranji Trophy: First-class matches between teams within each of the five major zones — Central, North, South, West and East — with the two top teams playing off in a grand final.
- Duleep Trophy: each of the five zone teams play in a four-

day match competition.
- Irani Cup: a five-day match between the Ranji Trophy winners and the Rest of India.

NEW ZEALAND
- Trans-Tasman Trophy: contested by Australia and New Zealand in test matches.
- National Bank. Series Trophy: test matches against visiting teams.
- National Bank Series Cup: one-day series against visiting teams.
- Shell Trophy: contested by the six first-class provincial teams in first- class cricket.
- Shell Cup: contested by all the first-class provincial teams in 50-over one-day cricket.
- Shell Super Max: contested by all the first-class provincial teams in Cricket Max (40-over games that comprise four IO-over innings, with the game being completed in three and a half hours).
- Hawke Cup: played for by the minor-associations.
- Shell Rose Bowl: New Zealand Women's Team contest against Australia.
- State Insurance Cup: 50-over matches contested by Auckland, Canterbury, Wellington, Otago, Northern Districts and Central Districts Women's Teams.

PAKISTAN
- Quaid-E-Azam Trophy: three-day first-class matches.
- PCB Patrons Trophy: three-day first-class matches.

SOUTH AFRICA
- Supersport Series: four-day first-class matches contested by the major provincial teams in first-class cricket (formerly

known as the Currie Cup and the Castle Cup): Border, Boland, Eastern Province, Griqualand West, Kwa Zulu-Natal, Free State, Transvaal (Gauteng), Western Province, Northwest, Easterns, Northerns.
- Standard Bank Cup: 50-over one-day competition.

SRI LANKA
- Mercantile Cricket Association Challenge Trophy: three-day first-class matches.

WEST INDIES
- Busta Clip: four-day first-class matches between Barbados, Jamaica, Leeward Islands, Trinidad and Tobago, Guyana and the Windward Islands.
- Red Stripe Bowl: 50-over competition.

ZIMBABWE
- Logan Cup: three-day first-class matches.

CHAPTER 18

Major Cricket Venues

Many great test and one-day internationals have been played on some wonderful grounds. Here are the major venues around the world.

AUSTRALIA
Adelaide	Adelaide Oval
Brisbane	Woolloongabba (The Gabba)
Hobart	Bellerive Oval (Tasmania)
Melbourne	MCG (Melbourne Cricket Ground)
Perth	WACA (Western Australian Cricket Association Ground)
Sydney	SCG (Sydney Cricket Ground)

BANGLADESH
Dhaka	Bangabandu National .Stadium

ENGLAND
Birmingham	Egbaston (Warwickshire)
Leeds	Headingley (Yorkshire)
London	Fosters Oval (Kennington, Surrey)
London	Lord's (St John's Wood, Middlesex)
Manchester	Old Trafford (Lancashire)
Nottingham	Trent Bridge (Nottinghamshire)

INDIA

Ahmedabad	Gujarat Stadium
Bangalore	Chinnaswamy Stadium
Mumbai (Bombay)	Wankhede Stadium
Calcutta	Eden Gardens
Cuttack	Barabari Stadium
Delhi	Feroz Shah Kotla
Hyderabad	Fateh Maidan
Kanour	Modi Stadium
Chennai (Madras)	Chepauk
Mohali	Punjab Cricket Association Stadium
Nagpur	VGA Ground

NEW ZEALAND

Auckland	Eden Park
Christchurch	Jade Stadium at Lancaster Park
Dunedin	Carisbrook
Hamilton	WestpacTrust Park
Napier	McLean Park
Wellington	Basin Reserve and Westpac Trust Stadium

PAKISTAN

Faisalabad	Iqbal Stadium
Karachi	The National Stadium
Lahore	The Gaddafi Stadium
Peshawar	Arbab Niaz Stadium
Rawalpindi	Rawalpindi Cricket Stadium
Sialkot	Jinnah Stadium

SOUTH AFRICA

Cape Town	Newlands (Western Province)
Durban	Kingsmead (Natal)

Johannesburg	New Wanderers (Transvaal)
Port Elizabeth	St George's Park (Eastern Province)
Pretoria	Centurion Park (Northern Transvaal)

SRI LANKA

Colombo	P. Saravanamuttli Stadium
Colombo	Colombo Cricket Club Ground
Colombo	R. Premadasa (Khettarama) Stadium
Galle	Galle International Stadium
Kandy	Asgiriya Stadium
Moratuwa	Tyronne Fernando Stadium

WEST INDIES

Antigua	St John's Recreation Ground, St John's
Barbados	Kensington Oval, Bridgetown
Guyana	Bourda, Georgetown
Jamaica	Sabina Park, Kingston
St Vincent	Arnos Vale, Kingstown
Trinidad	Queens Park, Port of Spain

ZIMBABWE

Bulawayo	Queens Sports Club
Harare	Harare Sports Club

CHAPTER 19

For the Record

Cricket statistics are an important and interesting part of the game. Test records are generally regarded as a guideline to a player's true ability, but one-day records are becoming increasingly important.

These figures are Sourced from The Wisden Cricketer's Almanac 2003 and Sir Richard Hadlee for the New Zealand records.

TEST BATTING (WORLD)

Highest test innings
952/6 Sri Lanka v India at Colombo, Sri Lanka, 1997-98
903/7 England v Australia at the Oval, London, England, 1938
849 England v West Indies at Kingston, Jamaica, 1929-30

Lowest test innings
26 New Zealand v England at Auckland, New Zealand, 1954-55
30 South Africa v England at Port Elizabeth, South Africa, 1895-96
30 South Africa v England at Birmingham, England, 1924

Highest individual test innings
375 Brian Lara - West Indies v England at St John's, Antigua, 1993-94
365 Garfield Sobers - West Indies v Pakistan at Kingston, Jamaica, 1957-58
364 Len Hutton - England v Australia at The Oval, London, England, 1938

Most runs in test cricket
11174 Allan Border (Australia) at an average of 50.56
10122 Sunil Gavaskar (India) at an average of 51.12
9600 Steve Waugh (Australia) 50.00

Most test centuries
34 Sunil Gavaskar (India)
30 Sachin Tendulkar (India)
29 Don Bradman (Australia)

Most runs in a test series
974 Don Bradman - Australia v England, 1930 (5 tests)
905 Walter Hammond - England v Australia, 1928-29 (5 tests)
839 Mark Taylor - Australia v England 1989 (6 tests)

MISCELLANEOUS RECORDS

Fastest test 50 (in 28 mins)
J.T. Brown
England v Australia at Melbourne, Australia, 1894-95

Fastest test 100 (in 70 mins)
Jack Gregory
Australia v South Africa at Johannesburg, South Africa, 1921-22

Fastest double 100 (in 214 mins)
Don Bradman
Australia v England at Leeds, England, 1930

Fastest triple century (in 288 mins)
Walter Hammond
England v New Zealand at Auckland, New Zealand, 1932-33

Most test runs in a day
309, Don Bradman
Australia v England at Leeds, England, 1930

Slowest test 100
557 mins, Mudassar Nazar
Pakistan v England at Lahore, Pakistan, 1977-78

WORLD RECORD TEST PARTNERSHIPS

1st wkt 413 Vinoo Mankad & Pankaj Roy - India v New Zealand at Madras, India, 1955-56
2nd wkt 576 Sanath Jayasuriya & Roshan Mahanama - Sri Lanka v India at Colombo, Sri Lanka, 1997-98
3rd wkt 467 Andrew Jones & Martin Crowe - New Zealand v Sri Lanka at Wellington, New Zealand, 1990-91
4th wkt 411 Peter May & Colin Cowdrey- England v West Indies at Birmingham, England, 1957
5th wkt 405 Sid Barnes & Don Bradman - Australia v England at Sydney, Australia, 1946-47
6th wkt 346 Jack Fingleton & Don Bradman - Australia v England at Melbourne, Australia, 1936-37
7th wkt 347 Denis Atkinson & Clairmonte Depeiza - West Indies v Australia at Bridgetown, Trinidad, 1954-55
8th wkt 313 Wasim Akram & Saqlain Mushtaq - Pakistan v Zimbabwe at Sheikhupura, Pakistan, 1996-97
9th wkt 195 Mark Boucher & Pat Symcox - South Africa v Pakistan at Johannesburg, South Africa, 1997-98
10th wkt 151 Brian Hastings & Richard Collinge - New Zealand v Pakistan at Auckland, New Zealand, 1972-73
151 Azhar Mahmood & Mushtaq Ahmed - Pakistan v South Africa at Rawalpindi, Pakistan, 1997-98

TEST BOWLING
Most wickets in a test innings
10-53 Jim Laker - England v Australia at Old Trafford, Manchester, England, 1956

10-74	Anil Kumble - India v Pakistan at Delhi, India, 1998-99
9-28	George Lohmann - England v South Africa at Johannesburg, South Africa, 1895-96
9-37	Jim Laker - England v Australia at Old Trafford, Manchester, England, 1956
9-52	Richard Hadlee - New Zealand v Australia at the Gabba, Brisbane, 1985-86

Most wickets in a test match

19-90	Jim Laker - England v Australia at Old Trafford, Manchester, England, 1956
17-159	Syd Barnes - England v South Africa at Johannesburg, South Africa, 1913-14
16-136	Narendra Hirwani - India v West Indies at Madras, India, 1987-88

Most wickets in a test series

49	Syd Barnes (4 tests) - England v South Africa, 1913-14
46	Jim Laker (5 tests) - England v Australia, 1956
44	Clarrie Grimmett (5 tests) - Australia v South Africa, 1935-36

Most bags of 5 wickets in a career

36	Richard Hadlee (New Zealand)
27	Ian Botham (England)
25	Wasim Akram (Pakistan)
24	Syd Barnes (England)
23	Dennis Lillee (Australia), Kapil Dev (India), Imran Khan (Pakistan)

Most bags of 10 wickets in a match

9	Richard Hadlee (New Zealand)
7	Dennis Lillee (Australia)
7	Syd Barnes (England)
7	Clarrie Grimmett (Australia)

Most test wickets in a career
519   Courtney Walsh (West Indies)
450   Shane Warne (Australia)
434   Kapil Dev (India)

TEST FIELDING
Most dismissals by a wicket-keeper in a test innings
7   Wasim Bari - Pakistan v New Zealand at Auckland, New Zealand, 1978-79
7   Bob Taylor - England v India at Bombay, India, 1979-80
7   Ian Smith - New Zealand v Sri Lanka at Hamilton, New Zealand, 1990-91

Most dismissals by a wicket-keeper in a test match
11   Jack Russell - England v South Africa at Johannesburg, South Africa, 1995-96
10   Bob Taylor - England v India at Bombay, India, 1979-80
10   Adam Gilchrist - Australia v New Zealand at Hamilton, New Zealand, 1999-2000

Most dismissals by a wicket-keeper in a test series
28   Rod Marsh - Australia v England, 1982-83 (5 tests)
27   Jack Russell - England v South Africa, 1995-96 (5 tests)
27   Ian Healy - Australia v England, 1997 (6 tests)

Most dismissals by a wicket-keeper in a test career
395   Ian Healy (Australia) in 119 tests
355   Rod Marsh (Australia) in 96 tests
270   Jeffrey Dujon (West Indies) in 79 tests

Most catches by a fielder in a test innings
5   Victor Richardson - Australia v South Africa at Durban, South Africa, 1935-36
5   Yajurvindra Singh - India v England at Bangalore, India, 1976-77

5	Mohammad Azharuddin - India v Pakistan at Karachi, Pakistan, 1989-90
5	Kris Srikkanth - India v Australia at Perth, Australia, 1991-92
5	Stephen Fleming - New Zealand v Zimbabwe at Harare, Zimbabwe, 1997-98

Most catches by a fielder in a test match

7	Greg Chappell - Australia v England at Perth, Australia, 1974-75
7	Yajurvindra Singh - India v England at Bangalore, India, 1976-77
7	Hashan Tillekeratne - Sri Lanka v New Zealand at Colombo, Sri Lanka, 1992-93
7	Stephen Fleming - New Zealand v Zimbabwe at Harare, Zimbabwe, 1997-98

Most catches by a fielder in a test career

173	Mark Waugh (Australia) in 125 tests.
157	Mark Taylor (Australia) in 104 tests
156	Allan Border (Australia) in 156 tests

Most catches in a test series

15	Jack Gregory - Australia v England, 1920-21
14	Greg Chappell - Australia v England, 1974-75

Most test match appearances

156	Allan Border (Australia)
148	Steve Waugh (Australia)
132	Courtney Walsh (West Indies)

NEW ZEALAND TEST RECORDS

Sourced from the records of Sir Richard Hadlee

Highest team test innings
671/4   v Sri Lanka at Wellington, New Zealand, 1990-91

Lowest team test innings
26   v England at Auckland, New Zealand, 1954-55

Highest individual test innings
299   Martin Crowe v Sri Lanka at Wellington, New Zealand, 1990-91
267   Bryan Young v Sri Lanka at Dunedin, New Zealand, 1996-97
259   Glenn Turner v West Indies at Georgetown, Guyana, 1971-72

Most runs in test cricket
5444   Martin Crowe (average of 45.36)
5334   John Wright (average of 37.82)
4217   Fleming (average of 36.35)

Most test centuries
17   Martin Crowe
12   John Wright
7   John R. Reid, Glenn Turner, Andrew Jones

Test partnerships
1st wkt 387   Glenn Turner & Terry Jarvis - v West Indies at Georgetown, Guyana, 1971-72
2nd wkt 241   John Wright & Andrew Jones - v England at Wellington, New Zealand, 1991-92
3rd wkt 467   Andrew Jones & Martin Crowe - v Sri Lanka at Wellington, New Zealand, 1990-91
4th wkt 243   Matthew Home & Nathan Astle - v Zimbabwe at Auckland, New Zealand, 1997-98

5th wkt	183	Mark Burgess & Robert Anderson - v Pakistan at Lahore, Pakistan, 1976-77
6th wkt	246	Jeff Crowe & Richard Hadlee - v Sri Lanka at Colombo, Sri Lanka, 1986-87
7th wkt	186	Warren Lees & Richard Hadlee - v Pakistan at Karachi, Pakistan, 1976-77
8th wkt	144	Chris Cairns & Dion Nash - v Zimbabwe at Harare, Zimbabwe, 2000-01
9th wkt	136	Ian Smith & Martin Snedden - v India at Auckland, New Zealand, 1989-90
10th wkt	151	Brian Hastings & Richard Collinge - v Pakistan at Auckland. New Zetland. 1972-73

Most wickets in an innings

9-52	Richard Hadlee - v Australia at Brisbane, Australia, 1985-86
7-23	Richard Hadlee - v India at Wellington, New Zealand, 1975-76
7-27	Chris Cairns - v West Indies at Hamilton, New Zealand, 1999-2000
7-52	Chris Pringle - v Pakistan at Faisalabad, Pakistan, 1990-91

Most wickets in a test match

15-123	Richard Hadlee - v Australia at Brisbane, Australia, 1985-86
12-149	Daniel Vettori - v Australia at Auckland, New Zealand, 1999-2000
11-58	Richard Hadlee - v India at Wellington, New Zealand, 1975-76
11-102	Richard Hadlee - v West Indies at Dunedin, New Zealand, 1979-80

Most test wickets
431	Richard Hadlee at an average of 22.29
197	Chris Cairns at an average of 28.80
160	Danny Morrison at an average of 34.68

Most wickets in a test series
33	Richard Hadlee - v Australia in Australia (3 tests), 1985-87
27	Bruce Taylor - v West Indies in the West Indies (4 tests), 1971-72

Most bags of 5 wickets in a test innings
36	Richard Hadlee
10	Danny Morrison
10	Chris Cairns

Most bags of 10 wickets in a test match
9	Richard Hadlee
1	Lance Cairns, Ewen Chatfield, John Bracewell, Dion Nash, Chris Pringle, Jack Cowie, Gary Troup, Daniel Vettori, Chris Cairns

Most dismissals by a wicket-keeper in a test innings
7	Ian Smith - v Sri Lanka at Hamilton, New Zealand, 1990-91
5	Roy Harford, Ken Wadsworth, Warren Lees, Adam Parore (3x), Ian Smith (2x)

Most dismissals by a wicket-keeper in a test match
8	Warren Lees - v Sri Lanka at Wellington, New Zealand, 1982-83
8	Ian Smith -v Sri Lanka at Hamilton. New Zealand 1990-91

Most dismissals by a wicket-keeper in a test series
23   Artie Dick - v South Africa, 1961-62

Most dismissals by a wicket-keeper in a test career
176   Ian Smith (168 catches, 8 stumpings)
152   Adam Parore (145 catches, 7 stumpings)
96   Ken Wadsworth (92 catches, 4 stumpings)

Most catches by a fielder in a test innings
5   Stephen Fleming - v Zimbabwe at Harare, Zimbabwe, 1997-98
4   Jeff Crowe - v West Indies at Bridgetown, Barbados, 1984-85
4   Martin Crowe - v West Indies at Kingston, Jamaica, 1984-85
4   Stephen Fleming - v Australia at Brisbane, Australia, 1997-98

Most catches by a fielder in a test match
7   Stephen Fleming - v Zimbabwe at Harare, Zimbabwe, 1997-98
6   Bryan Young - v Pakistan at Auckland, New Zealand, 1993-94
6   Stephen Fleming - v Australia at Brisbane, 1997-98

Most catches by a fielder in a test career
86   Stephen Fleming
71   Martin Crowe
64   Jeremy Coney

Most test appearances
86   Richard Hadlee
82   John Wright
77   Martin Crowe

ONE-DAY BATTING
Highest team score in an innings
398/5	Sri Lanka v Kenya at Kandy, Sri Lanka, 1995-96	
376/2	India v New Zealand at Hyderabad, India, 1999-2000	
373/6	India v Sri Lanka at Taunton, England, 1999	

Lowest team innings
43	Pakistan v West Indies at Capetown, South Africa, 1992-93 (19.5 overs)
45	Canada v England at Old Trafford, Manchester, England, 1979 (40.3 overs)
38	Zimbabwe v Sri Lanka, Colombo, Sri Lanka, 2001-02 (15.4 overs)

Highest individual score
194	Saeed Anwar - Pakistan v India at Chennai, 1996-97
189	Viv Richards - West Indies v England at Old Trafford, Manchester, England, 1984
189	JayaSuriya, Sri Lanka V India at Sharjah 2000-01
188	Gary Kirsten - South Africa v United Arab Emirates at Rawalpindi, Pakistan, 1995-96

Most runs in a career
11544	Sachin Tendulkar (India)
9378	Mohammad Azharuddin (India)
8803	Aravinda De Silva (Sri Lanka)

Most centuries
33	Sachin Tendulkar (India)
19	Sourav Ganguly (India)
19	Saeed Anwar (Pakistan)

One-day partnerships
1st wkt	258	Sourav Ganguly & Sachin Tendulkar - India Kenya, Paarl, Australia 2001-02
2nd wkt	331	Sachin Tendulkar & Rahul Dravid - India v New Zealand at Hyderabad, India, 1999 - 2000
3rd wkt	237	Rahul Dravid & Sachin Tendulkar - India v Kenya at Bristol, England, 1999

4th wkt	275	M. Azharuddin & Ajay Jadeja - India v Zimbabwe at Cuttack, India, 1997-98
5th wkt	223	M. Azharuddin & Ajay Jadeja - India v Sri Lanka at Colombo, Sri Lanka, 1997-98
6th wkt	161	Maurice Odumbe & A.V. Vadher - Kenya v Sri Lanka at Southampton, England, 1999
7th wkt	130	Andrew Flower & Heath Streak, Zimbabwe v England, Harare, Zimbabwe 2001-02.
8th wkt	119	Paul Reiffel & Shane Warne - Australia v South Africa at Port Elizabeth, South Africa, 1993-94
9th wkt	126	Kapil Dev & Syed Kirmani - India v Zimbabwe at Tunbridge Wells, England, 1983
10th wkt	106	Viv Richards & Michael Holding - West Indies v England at Manchester, England, 1984

ONE-DAY BOWLING AND FIELDING

Best bowling in an innings

8-19	Chaminda Vaas, Sri Lanka, V Zimbabwe, at Colombo Sri Lanka, 2001-02
7-30	M Murali Tharam, Sri Lanka V India, Sharjah, UAE, 2000-01
7-36	Waqar Younis, Pakistan v England, Leeds, England 2001

Most wickets in a career

479	Wasim Akram (Pakistan)
395	Waqar Younis (Pakistan)
299	Anil Kumble (India)

Most dismissals by a wicket-keeper in an innings

6	Adam Gilchrist, Australia v South Africa at Newlands, Cape Town, South Africa, 1999-2000
6	Alec Stewart, England v Zimbabwe at Manchester, England, 2000
6	Ridley Jacobs, West Indies V Sri Lanka at Colombo, Sri Lanka, 2001-02 2001-02

5   The following players have made five dismissals in an innings: Rod Marsh (Australia), Guy de Alwis, Hashan Tillekeratne, Romesh Kaluwitharana (Sri Lanka), Adam Parore (New Zealand), Moin Khan, Rashid Latif (Pakistan), David Richardson, Mark Boucher (South Africa), Syed Kirmani, Nayan Mongia, Sadanani Viswanath, Kiran More (India), Andy Flower (Zimbabwe), Jimmy Adams, Courtney Browne, Ridley Jacobs (West Indies)

Most dismissals by a wicket-keeper in a career
257   Moin Khan (Pakistan)
236   Adam Gilchrist (Australia)
234   Ian Healy (Australia)

Most catches by a fielder in an innings
5   Jonty Rhodes - South Africa v West Indies at Bombay, India, 1993-94
4   Richie Richardson, Phil Simmons, Carl Hooper (West Indies), Kepler Wessels (South Africa), Mark Taylor (Australia), Sunil Gavaskar, Mohammad Azharuddin, Sachin Tendulkar (India), Salim Malik (Pakistan), Ken Rutherford (New Zealand) and Guy Whitall (Zimbabwe)

Most catches by a fielder in a career
156   Mohammad Azharuddin (India)
127   Allan Border (Australia)
111   Steve Waugh (Australia)

Most appearances in one-day cricket
343   Wasim Akram (Pakistan)
334   Mohammad Azharuddin (India)
325   Steve Waugh (Australia)

NEW ZEALAND ONE-DAY RECORDS

Sourced from the records of Sir Richard Hadlee

Highest team innings
349/9 v India at Rajket, India, 1999-2000

Lowest team innings
64 v Pakistan at Sharjah, United Arab Emirates, 1985-86

Most runs in a career
4704 Martin Crowe (average 38.55)
3891 John Wright (average 26.45)
3720 Nathan Astle (average 35.09)

Most centuries
8 Nathan Astle
4 Martin Crowe
3 Glenn Turner, Stephen Fleming

One-day partnerships
1st wkt 155 Bryan Young & Nathan Astle v Pakistan at Mohali, Pakistan, 1996-97
2nd wkt 130 Bruce Edgar & Martin Crowe v India at Brisbane, Australia, 1985-86
3rd wkt 180 Adam Parore & Ken Rutherford v India at Baroda, Pakistan, 1994-95
4th wkt 168 Lee Germon & Chris Harris v Australia at Madras, India, 1995-96
5th wkt 148 Roger Twose & Chris Cairns v Australia at Cardiff, Wales, 1999
6th wkt 130 Ken Wadsworth & Bevan Congdon v Australia at Christchurch, New Zealand, 1973-74
7th wkt 115 Adam Parore & Lee Germon v Pakistan at Sharjah, United Arab Emirates, 1996-97
8th wkt 69 Adam Parore & Dion Nash v South Africa at Brisbane, Australia, 1997-98
9th wkt 63 Richard Hadlee & Gary Troup v Australia at Brisbane, Australia, 1982-83

10th wkt   65   Martin Snedden & Ewen Chatfield v Sri Lanka
                 at Derby, England, 1983

Best bowling in an innings
10-2-22-5   Matthew Hart - v West Indies at Goa, India,
             1994-95
7-1-23-5   Richard Collinge - v India at Christchurch, New
             Zealand, 1975-76
10.1-4-25-5 Richard Hadlee - v Sri Lanka at Bristol, England,
             1983

Most economical bowling in a match
10-4-8-1   Ewen Chatfield - v Sri Lanka at Dunedin, New
             Zealand, 1982-83
12-6-10-0   Richard Hadlee - v East Africa at Birmingham,
             England, 1975
10-6-10-0   Lance Cairns - v Sri Lanka at Dunedin, New
             Zealand, 1983

Most wickets in a career
158   Richard Hadlee (average 21.56)
145   Chris Harris (average 34.82)
140   Ewen Chatfield (average 25.84)

Most dismissals by a wicket-keeper in an innings
5   Adam Parore - v West Indies at Goa, India, 1994-95
4   Warren Lees, Adam Parore, Tony Blain, Lee Germon

Most catches by a fielder in an innings
4   Ken Rutherford - v India at Napier, New Zealand,
     1994-95
4   John Bracewell (substitute fielder) - v Australia at
Adelaide, Australia, 1980-81

Most one-day appearances
156   Chris Harris
149   John Wright
143   Martin Crowe

CHAPTER 20

Cricketing Terms

To understand and appreciate the game of cricket, many terms, sayings and laws need to be explained. These are used by the players, umpires, administrators, commentators and spectators.

ABDOMINAL PROTECTOR — Also called the box. This is a protective device used by a batsman, a wicket-keeper or a close-in fielder to protect the groin or genital area.

ADMINISTRATOR — A person who serves on a cricket board and whose duty is to ensure that all aspects of the game are managed effectively and efficiently.

AGGREGATE — Total number of runs scored, wickets taken or catches completed by a player in a given period of time, e.g. for the season or his or her career to dare

AGRICULTURAL SHOT — Term use to be describe an unconventional cross-bat swipe at the ball.

ALL-ROUNDER — A player who has at least two skills of near equal ability, e.g. a specialist batsman who bats as high as number six and who is also regarded as a specialist bowler. Players such as Sir Garfield Sobers, Ian Botham, Kapil Dev, Imran Khan and Sir Richard Hadlee were regarded as genuine all-rounders. They were also competent fielders.

ALTERING A DECISION: Law 27 — An umpire may change his decision — for example, reverse a dismissal, change a signalled four to a six or change a leg bye to runs — provided he does so quickly. The captain of the fielding team may ask the umpire to withdraw their appeal, giving the umpire the opportunity to change his decision.

AMATEUR — A player who receives no financial reward. He or she may be reimbursed for travelling or meal expenses.

ANALYSIS — This relates to the bowler's performance in terms of the overs bowled, maiden overs completed, runs conceded, wickets taken in an innings, match, season or during a career. This is usually shown as, for example, 20-4-52-6.

APPEALS: Law 27 — If the fielding side believes that a batsman is out, they can appeal to the umpire with a call of, 'How's that?' It covers all ways of being out, unless a specific way of getting out is stated by the person asking. Although the ball is dead when 'over' is called, an appeal can still be made before the first ball of the next over, provided the bails have not been removed by both umpires after 'time' has been called, either for the close of play or for a lunch or tea break.

ARC — Generally refers to the flight of the ball bowled by a spin bowler who applies overspin to the ball. The well-flighted ball into the breeze drops onto the pitch at a sharper than expected angle, sometimes causing the batsman to misjudge his stroke and offer a catch. The arc of the ball has deceived the batsman.

ARMGUARD — A piece of padding used to protect the batsman's forearm and prevent injury if struck from a fast rising ball from a fast bowler.

ARTIFICIAL PITCH — Any type of surface that is not grass, e.g. concrete, matting, Astroturf, rubber or other types of artificial grass.

ASHES — This is a trophy played for by Australia and England in a test match series. The origin of the term goes back to 1882, when Australia defeated England by seven runs at the Oval, therefore beating England, the inventor of cricket, for the first time in England. On the following day, the *Sporting Times* published an obituary for English cricket.

> In affectionate remembrance of English Cricket which died at the Oval, 29th August 1882, deeply lamented by a large circle of sorrowing friends and acquaintances, R.I.P.
> N.B. The body will be cremated and the Ashes taken to Australia.

The following winter, when England toured Australia, England won two of the three tests. Several women burnt a set of bails and then sealed the ashes in a small urn. This they presented to the English captain, the Hon. Ivo Bligh, later Lord Darnley, who retained the urn until his death in 1927. The urn, which was given to the MCC by Lord Darnley's widow, can now be seen at the museum at Lord's.

ATTACK — Often used when referring to the bowling battery available to the captain to use at his discretion. The bowling attack may have three fast bowlers and two spin bowlers. The term is also used when a batsman attacks the bowlers and looks to score his runs quickly.

AVERAGE — This is the figure that determines a batsman's or bowler's overall performance. Runs scored are divided by the number of times a batsman is out and runs conceded by a bowler by the number of wickets taken.

AWAY SWINGER — Term used to describe a bowler's outswinger.

BACK CUT — A stroke played by the batsman behind point on the off side. It is often played late, hence the term 'late cut'.

BACKING UP — The non-striker is said to be backing up when he advances a few paces up the pitch after the delivery of the ball, with the expectation of a possible run. This makes it easier to steal a run or short single. Backing up also applies to a fielder who covers another in case he misses the ball. This often happens when the ball is returned to the wicket-keeper. A fielder will be in a position behind the wicket-keeper.

BACK OF A LENGTH — A ball pitching short of a good length forcing the batsman to play a defensive shot at the ball.

BACK-SPIN — An underspin of the ball, usually from slow bowlers, causing the ball to come off the pitch more slowly.

BACKWARD — The field placements on either side of the wicket behind the line square of the batsman, e.g. backward point on the offside or backward square leg on the leg side.

BAG OF WICKETS — The bowler has captured five or more wickets in an innings.

BAILS: *Law 8* — The two bails are placed on top of the three stumps/wickets at each end of the pitch or wicket. They are 11.1 centimetres (4-3/8 inches) long and, when positioned on top of the stumps, must not project more than 1.3 centimetres (½ inch) above them. For the batsman to be out, the bail or bails have to fall off the top of the stumps. He is not out if the bails are disturbed but not dislodged.

BALL: *Law 5* — The official match ball should be made of four pieces of leather on the outside with a cork and rubber centre wrapped in string. The outer casing is stitched. It should weigh not less than 155.9 grams (5 ½ ounces) or more than 163 grams (5½ ounces). It should measure not less than 216 millimetres (9 inches) in circumference.

In most grades of cricket, a two-piece leather ball is used. Sometimes youngsters will use a composition or nylon ball in the backyard.

For all test and first-class matches a red ball is used, but in most one-day internationals and in all day-night matches a white ball is used.

BALL COUNTER — Used by the umpires to count the number of balls bowled in an over. Some devices will also record the number of overs bowled.

BALL DOCTORING: *Law 42.4* — A term used when the fielding side deliberately changes the original condition of the ball by using artificial substances such as creams, fingernails, bottle tops, etc. The umpire can change the ball and report the offence to the officials. Ball doctoring is deemed to be unfair play.

BASHER — A colloquial term to describe a batsman who plays positively with a mixed array of strokes, including slog shots. Often referred to as a slogger, with the ball being hit to cow corner.

BAT: *Law 6* — A quality cricket bat is made of English willow. Other bats are made from Indian Kashmir willow. A bat should not exceed 108 millimetres (4¼ inches) at its widest point and 965 millimetres (38 inches) in length. The handle is made of cane and has a rubber grip.

BAT COVER — Most players like to look after their bats, which can be worth hundreds of dollars. A bat cover will protect the face of the bat from damage when not in use.

BAT-PAD — A fielding position usually a couple of metres in front of the batsman. It is also called silly mid-off (on the off side) or silly mid-on (on the leg side). It is also referred to as the suicide position.

BATSMAN — The person who takes strike against the bowler. He uses a bat made of willow and he is well protected with padding around the legs and other parts of the body. He wears batting gloves and his job is to score runs and keep his wicket intact.

BATSMAN RETIRING HURT: *Law 2.9* — If the batsman is injured or feels ill, he may consult the umpires and retire hurt and another batsman will come out to bat. At the fall of a wicket, he may return to continue his innings.

BATSMAN'S PARADISE — The pitch is a good one to bat on; the ball comes onto the bat and stroke play is easy.

BATSMAN UNFAIRLY STEALING A RUN: *Law 42.12* — If the batsman tries to steal a run by leaving his crease at the bowler's end before the ball is bowled, it is deemed to be unfair play. The batsman can also be run out by the bowler, but the bowler usually gives the batsman a warning first.

BATTER — A common term in the 18th century in the north of England, still used on occasions today to describe the batsman.

BATTING AVERAGE — A batsman's batting average is calculated by dividing the number of runs scored by the number of times he has been dismissed, e.g. 590 runs scored in the season but dismissed 10 times gives him an average of 59 runs per innings.

BATTING CREASE: *Law 9* — This is the line that the batsman stands on when he faces the bowler. If he has his foot and/or bat outside the crease, he can be given out run out or slumped. It is also called the popping crease. This line will also determine whether the bowler has bowled a fair delivery. The bowler must have part of his front foot grounded or raised behind the line at the point of releasing the ball, otherwise a no ball will be called by the umpire. (See diagram on p. 76.)

BEAMER — A full-pitched delivery aimed at the batsman's head, either intentionally or unintentionally. If this happens intentionally, the umpires will consider the action to be dangerous and unfair play. The bowler will be reported and dealt with under any special code of conduct rules. If it is unintentional, the bowler will usually apologise. Also called a bean ball.

BEATEN — When a batsman attempts to play at a ball and misses it.

BEATEN ALL ENDS UP — When a batsman plays at a ball and is completely deceived by it.

BENEFIT SEASON — A player will receive a benefit season after years of loyal service, usually 10 years. It is an acknowledgement of that player's contribution to the game and to their club. He can form a committee and organise various fund-raising activities to secure his future. He will sometimes receive the gate proceeds from a specific match or matches. Dinners, golf days, auctions and raffles are common revenue earners.

BITE — The amount of spin a bowler can extract from the pitch, often getting the ball to lift sharply. Also referred to as spin, bounce or turn.

BLADE — The front part of the bat that strikes the ball.

BLINDER — Slang term for a magnificent catch taken in the field, usually a one-handed diving catch.

BLIND SPOT — A small area of the pitch where, if the ball bounces here, the batsman may doubt whether to play forward or back.

BLOB — Another term for a batsman scoring a duck or no runs.

BLOCK — Describes the pitch area, a batsman's guard or a batsman playing a defensive shot at the ball.

BLOCK HOLE — The block hole is made by the batsman on or just behind the popping crease, when he marks the position of his guard, given to him by the umpire.

BLOCK HOLER — When the bowler lands the ball in the area where the batsman has marked his guard.

BODYLINE — Tactics used by England's fast bowlers during the 1932-33 Ashes tour of Australia, in which a barrage of short-pitched deliveries were aimed at the batsman's upper body to prevent him scoring runs. Some batsmen ended up taking evasive action while others popped up a catch to the close-in leg-side fielders known as the leg trap. This type of bowling was later outlawed.

BOSIE — A type of ball bowled, named after its Australian inventor, B.J.T. Bosanquet, where the ball bowled by a leg-spinner breaks from the off stump towards the leg stump. This delivery is also called a googly or a wrong 'un.

BOTTOM EDGE — An involuntary stroke played by the batsman in which the ball makes contact with the bottom of the bat. This often happens when a batsman has to dig out an attempted yorker or full-pitched delivery from a bowler.

BOUNCER — A short-pitched delivery, usually bowled by a faster bowler, which rises sharply at the batsman. The ball is directed at the upper part of the batsman's body, but usually passes over the head. Also called a bumper.

BOUNDARIES: *Law 19* — The outside limit of the playing area. Most boundaries are about 75 metres (245 feet) for a first-class match but will vary in other types of cricket, depending on the size of the ground available.

When the ball crosses the boundary line, four runs are scored and the umpire will signal and say 'Boundary four'. If the ball goes over the boundary line on the full, six runs are scored and credited to the batsman. The umpire will signal and say 'Boundary six'.

BOUNDARY FLAG — Some boundary lines are marked with little flags to clearly define the line for the players and umpires.

BOUNDARY LINE — For all international, first-class, club matches and other grades of cricket, a white line is painted on the ground to clearly define the boundary line. Some grounds may use a rope.

BOWL — To deliver the ball in a fair way as prescribed by the Laws of Cricket. In 1744, all bowling was underarm. In 1835 the law was altered to allow round-arm bowling. In 1864, overarm bowling was permitted.

BOWLED: *Law 30* — A batsman is out bowled when the ball hits the wickets and the bail or bails fall off, even if the ball hits the bat or the batsman first.

BOWLER — The player who delivers the ball from the bowler's end. He must bowl the ball with an overarm action and it must be a fair delivery in the eyes of the umpire. He will bowl six legal balls in an over.

In the early days of cricket, the underarm delivery was legal. Women invented the overarm and round-arm delivery; since that time overarm has been accepted as the only way to bowl and underarm was eventually outlawed.

BOWLER'S MARKER — The plastic or metal disc used by the bowler to mark the start of his run-up. The umpire usually looks after the disc and offers it to the next bowler.

BOWLING AVERAGE — A bowler's bowling average is calculated by dividing the number of runs conceded from his bowling by the number of wickets he has taken, e.g. 1200 runs conceded in a season, with 50 wickets captured gives him a bowling average of 24 runs per wicket.

BOWLING CREASE: *Law 9* — The bowling crease is in line with the stumps and is 2.6 metres (8 feet 8 inches) in length, with the three stumps or wickets placed in the centre. Before the no ball law changed, the bowler had to have some part of his back foot grounded behind the line when the ball was released. Today, part of the bowler's front foot must be grounded or raised behind the popping or batting crease at the point of delivery. (See diagram on p. 76.)

BOWLING FAST, SHORT-PITCHED DELIVERIES: *Law 42.8* — If, in the umpire's opinion, a fast bowler is bowling these sorts of deliveries persistently, he can take preventative action by warning the bowler to stop. If the bowler persists after two warnings, the umpire can remove the bowler from the bowling crease for the rest of that innings.

BOWLING FAST, HIGH, FULLY PITCHED DELIVERIES: *Law 42.9* — This sort of bowling is deemed to be unfair and dangerous. The umpire will call 'No ball' and carry out the procedure as for Law 42.8.

BOWLING IN TANDEM — Two bowlers bowling from opposite ends for a period of time to good effect; e.g. two fast bowlers or two spin bowlers.

BOWLING MACHINE — A machine designed to project the ball at the batsman for batting practice. The machine can bowl fast, slow, swing and spin deliveries. A bowler is sometimes termed a bowling machine if he can send down, for example, 20 accurate overs in a day.

BOX — Name given to a protective device to cover the batsman's genital area. Also known as an abdominal protector. Wicket-keepers and close-in fielders also wear boxes.

BREAK BACK — A sharp off-break delivery with the ball turning from the off stump to the leg stump.

BUMP BALL — A ball that the batsman hits hard into the ground and is then caught. When fielded by the fielder close to the wicket, a bump ball gives the appearance of being a catch.

BUMPER — Also called a bouncer. A fast, short-pitched delivery aimed to intimidate the batsman and induce a false shot and get him out. The batsman will duck under, sway out of the way of the ball or attempt to play a hook shot. If the umpire believes that the bowler is persistently bowling short, he can warn the bowler. If the bowler does it again, he will receive another warning and the captain is advised. If the bowler offends again, he is not allowed to bowl again in the same innings.

BUNSEN BURNER — A colloquial term for a pitch that offers the spin bowler plenty of assistance. It rhymes with turner.

BYE: *Law 26* — Byes are runs scored from a ball that passes the wickets or stumps without touching the bat or batsman and is missed by the wicket-keeper. If the ball touches any part of the batsman, but not the bat or hands in contact with the bat, the runs scored will be leg byes.

CALLING — To avoid a careless run out, a batsman should use one of three calls after playing a shot: yes, if there is a run; no, if there is no run; and wait, followed by a yes or no call, depending on the situation.

CAPTAIN — RESPONSIBILITIES, UNFAIR PLAY: *Law 42.1* — The captain is elected or appointed to lead the team and set an example of the standards expected. He will be required to make many decisions before and during the match. He is responsible for ensuring that all players play the game in the true spirit and comply with the Laws of Cricket. (See Chapter 9.)

CARRIES HIS BAT — This is when an opening batsman bats through to the completion of the team's innings and leaves not out.

CASTLE — Colloquial term used for the wickets or set of stumps.

CAUGHT: *Law 32* — A batsman is caught out if a ball from the stroke of the batsman is caught by a fielder without the ball first touching the ground.

CAUGHT BEHIND — A batsman being caught by the wicket-keeper.

CENTRE — A guard or block taken by the batsman so that he can position himself in his stance on the line from middle stump at one end of the pitch to middle stump at the other end.

CENTURY — The scoring of 100 runs by one batsman.

CESSATION OF PLAY: *Law 17* — The umpire at the bowler's end can call 'Time' when there is an interval, an interruption in play, at the end of the day's play or when the match is over. The bails are removed and play ceases.

CHANCE — The batsman has given the fielding team an opportunity to get him out and they have failed to take advantage of it by dropping a catch or missing a run out or stumping.

CHANGE BOWLER — A bowler brought on to bowl after the main strike bowlers have completed their opening spell. He is called the first change bowler. The term is also used for a part-time bowler who may be used to try and break a batting partnership with a different variety of bowling.

CHANGING THE CONDITION OF THE BALL: *Law 42.5* — The fielding side is allowed to polish or shine the ball but not to rub artificial substances into it. They may use a cloth to dry a wet ball or to remove mud, but no one is allowed to rub the ball on the ground. If, in their opinion, the ball has been tampered with, the umpires can change it for another that is in similar condition to the original ball before the law was contravened.

CHEEKY SINGLE — When a batsman moves very quickly when running between the wickets to complete a risky run.

CHERRY — Term used for the new ball because it is shiny and red.

CHEST GUARD/PROTECTOR — Piece of padded equipment used by the batsman to protect his chest area against fast rising balls.

CHINAMAN — A left-arm bowler's off-break to a right-handed batsman. The ball spins from the off stump towards the leg stump. Named after Achong, a Chinese-West Indian who played for the West Indies in the 1930s. An English batsman was heard to have said, 'I have just been bowled by a chinaman.'

CHOP — A stroke from the batsman in the form of a late cut, bringing the bat down sharply on the ball just as it is about to pass the batsman on the off side.

CHUCKER — A bowler who has been deemed by the umpire to have thrown the ball while trying to bowl a legitimate delivery.

CLEAN BOWLED — When a batsman is comprehensively beaten and bowled.

CLIP — To strike the ball firmly off the toes into the on side.

CLOSE — To declare the innings closed with batsmen still intact.

CLOSE FIELD — The fielding positions close to the batsman, i.e. slips, gully, short legs, silly point, bat-pad (silly mid-on or silly mid-off).

CLOSE OF PLAY — The time arranged for play to finish. This will vary according to the type of game and the country. In most matches, stumps are drawn at 6 p.m. or when the minimum number of overs in a day's play have been completed after the scheduled finishing time.

CODE OF CONDUCT: *Law 42.13* — Relates to unfair play; in international matches, a match referee will enforce any breaches of the Laws of Cricket or relevant playing conditions that apply to the match. Generally relates to player abuse, dissent shown to an umpire's decision, excessive short- pitched bowling, slow over rates, etc.

CONDITIONS — The state of the ground and the weather. Also applies to the terms agreed upon by both teams before a game and by both participating countries before a tour begins.

CONKER — A colloquial term used for the ball. Sometimes the ball is also called the 'nut', or the 'pill'.

COUNTY CRICKET — Cricket played in England between the 18 major counties. It includes first-class and one-day cricket competitions.

COVER DRIVE — An attacking stroke off the front foot with the batsman looking to hit the ball into the cover region on the off side.

COVERING THE PITCH: *Law 11* — Before and during test, first-class and other types of cricket, the pitch will be covered to prevent rain damage. Also covered are the bowler run-ups and foot holes. The pitch is also covered at the end of the day's play.

COVER POINT — Fielding position on the off side about 20 metres from the batsman, square of the wicket.

COVERS — Usually canvas or plastic sheeting used to cover the pitch and playing area when it rains. Sometimes mobile covers on wheels are used to protect the pitch area. Also relates to a fielding position square of the wicket on the off side, about 20 metres from the batsman.

COW SHOT/COW CORNER — Cross-bat stroke or swipe at the ball by the batsman, with the ball being hit in the air to the wide mid-on region.

CRADLE — A cradle-shaped implement used by fieldsmen for slip catching practice. When the ball is thrown into the cradle, it comes off quickly and at unexpected angles.

CREASES — White lines painted on the pitch to show the batting and bowling creases as defined by the Laws of Cricket. See diagram on page 76.

CREEPER — A ball that shoots along the ground.

CRICKET MAX — A form of cricket developed by former New Zealand cricketer Martin Crowe, to add excitement and action to the game. Special rules apply, including doubling the score of a batsman if he hits the ball into the max zone; e.g. a six becomes 12 runs, four becomes eight and running two becomes four. A match may consist of two 10-over innings, with the game being completed within three and a half hours. No fielder can be positioned in the zone when the ball is bowled. If a bowler bowls a no ball, the batsman gets a free hit to the next delivery. A bowler is allowed to bowl a maximum of four overs during the match.

CROSS-BAT SHOT — A swipe shot that is made across the flight of the ball from off to leg, sending the ball anywhere on the leg side. The sweep or lap shots are common cross-bat shots that are sometimes called cow shots.

CRUMBLING PITCH OR WICKET — A very dry pitch, the surface of which breaks up or crumbles, owing to general wear and tear. The spin bowler will prosper on such a pitch because the ball will spin and bounce, sometimes unpredictably.

CURATOR — The groundsman or the person who prepares the pitch and general playing conditions.

CUT — A bowler can cut the ball by using his fingers to pull down the side of the ball, causing it to rotate in the air. When the ball hits the pitch, it will cut away from or towards the batsman. The term also describes a stroke where the batsman hits over the top of the ball to backward point on the offside.

CUTTER — A ball that is spun by the bowler by dragging the fingers down the back of the ball and towards one side. The ball will rotate through the air and, when it hits the pitch, it will grip and turn towards the batsman (off-cutter) or away from a right-handed batsman (leg-cutter).

CUT UP — Term used when the pitch changes its condition through wear and tear.

DANCE — When batting against a spin bowler, a batsman uses his feet to get to the pitch of the ball.

DANGER AREA; *Law 42.11* — This is an area 60 centimetres (2 feet) wide running for 30 centimetres (I foot) on either side of the line from one I middle stump to the other, and beginning 1.5 metres (5 feet) in front of the popping crease. If a bowler, in his follow through, lands in this area, the umpire is obliged to tell him to keep off because he is damaging the pitch and this is unfair to the batsman. If a bowler keeps infringing in this area, he can be removed from the bowling crease for the remainder of that innings.

DARTS — When the ball moves quickly off the seam from a fast bowler or when a spinner's faster delivery is bowled at a flatter trajectory.

DASHER — Term used to describe a batsman who plays attacking strokes throughout his innings. He scores his runs very quickly with cut and pull shots, along with drives, lofted shots and pushes.

DEAD BALL: *Law 23* — The ball is deemed to be dead when, in the umpire's opinion:

it has finally settled in the hands of the wicket-keeper or bowler,

- it has reached or crossed the boundary line,
- it has lodged in the dress or equipment of a batsman or in the clothing of an umpire,

- the umpire has called 'Over' or 'Time',
- a batsman is out,
- there has been unfair play or serious injury to a player,
- the batsman is not ready to take strike,
- the ball accidentally falls out of the bowler's hand before he delivers it,
- the bails are dislodged before the bowler delivers the ball,
- or the batsman decides to steal a run during the bowler's run-up, unless the bowler throws the ball at either wicket.

A ball does not become dead when it strikes the umpire or when the wicket is broken (unless the batsman is out) or when an unsuccessful appeal is made.

DEAD BAT — The batsman has played a defensive shot at the ball, hitting it into the ground a metre or so in front of him. This is a very common shot when a batsman is looking to save the match and has no interest in scoring runs.

DECK — Another term used for the pitch, as in 'The deck has played well today'.

DECLARATION OF AN INNINGS: *Law 14* — The batting captain may declare the innings closed at any time during a match, except in a one-day match. When a team declares, the opposing team will take their turn to bat.

DEEP — This is the part of the field away from the pitch and near the boundary.

DEFENCE — When a batsman offers a stroke at the ball but has no intention of trying to score runs.

DELIVERY — Another term for bowling the ball.

DEVIL — A wicket or pitch is said 'to have some devil in it' when it is lively and the batsman finds batting difficult.

DIG IN — A batsman sets out to consolidate the innings and remain at the crease for long periods of time, rather than trying to dominate the bowler and score runs.

DINNER — The break between innings in a day-night match.

DIRECT HIT — The fieldsman has hit the stumps without the assistance of the wicket-keeper at one end or the bowler at the other end. Sometimes a direct hit will bring about the dismissal of the batsman with a run out.

DIVOTS — Pieces cut out of the pitch by the action of batsmen or bowlers.

DOCTORING THE BALL — see 'ball doctoring'.

DONKEY DROP — A high, slow, full-tossed delivery bowled by a lob bowler, designed to fall on top of the stumps behind the batsman or to induce the batsman to hit a catch.

DOOSRA — The name of Pakistan off-spinner Saqlain Mushtaq's mystery ball that becomes his leg-spinner. An Urdu word meaning 'the other one'.

DOT BALL — A ball bowled from which the batting team hasn't scored.

DOUBLE-WICKET CRICKET — Two teams of two players playing against each other. Special rules apply as to the duration of the match and how many overs a player must bowl. Both teams have the benefit of nine other fieldsmen.

DRAG — When the bowler's back foot slides along the ground in the act of delivering the ball. It also refers to the batsman who may drag the ball back onto the stumps and be out bowled.

DRAW — A match is drawn when the team batting second still has at least one wicket intact and has not scored the accumulated total runs of the team batting first, or when the team bowling last has failed to capture all 10 wickets of the team batting second when the scheduled conclusion time of the match is reached. The match is unfinished.

Draw also refers to a shot played by the batsman when the front foot is raised high and the ball is hit or glanced between the legs.

DRESSING ROOM — Each team has a dressing room where they change and prepare for the match. Some provide a private viewing area of the field. At all first-class grounds, there is an attendant who looks after the players and their equipment.

DRINKS BREAK — The fielding team is allowed a drinks or liquid refreshments break, usually midway through a session's play. In normal conditions, a drinks break occurs one hour after play has begun. They usually last about five minutes and the twelfth man and, in some cases, other assistants, will bring a tray of drinks (usually water or energy beverages) onto the field. In some hot countries, there may be a drinks break every 40 minutes. The captain can decline to take a drinks break but in hot conditions all players are aware of the importance of maintaining their fluid intake. A batsman or bowler who has been on the field for a long time may ask for a drink.

DRIVE — A stroke played by the batsman with power as he strikes the ball forward of the wicket.

DROP — In fielding, to miss a catch. In batting, a position in the batting order; e.g. at the fall of the first wicket, the next batsman is referred to as first drop.

DROP ONE SHORT — In fast bowling, to fire in a short-pitched delivery at the batsman with the ball directed at the chest or head area.

DUCK — A score of nought by the batsman. In the scorebook it appears as an 0, which looks like a duck's egg. Also refers to a batsman who may take evasive action from a bouncer and duck under the ball.

ECB — England and Wales Cricket Board, which governs county cricket.

EDGE — The perimeter of the bat. The inside edge is the closest to the batsman's body when he plays a straight bat shot at the ball. The outside edge is the opposite side of the bat and the bottom edge is the end or the toe of the bat.

EIGHTS CRICKET — Two teams of eight players with special rules applying as to the duration of the match, with bowling and fielding restrictions.

ELEVEN — A cricket team is sometimes referred to as the playing XI.

EQUATION — Used in one-day matches to refer to the run rate per over that is required to win a match.

EXPRESS — A very fast bowler is said to bowl express deliveries.

EXTRAS — Runs added to the batting team's score that are not made by the batsman. They represent penalties incurred by the fielding side, e.g. wides, no balls, byes, leg byes. Also called sundries.

FACE — Describes the blade or front of the bat. The batsman is also said to face the bowler, meaning the batsman is taking strike and will receive the ball from the bowler.

FACEGUARD — Attached to the front of the helmet to protect the batsman's face from a rising delivery.

FALL — The number of runs scored by a team at the dismissal of each batsman in an innings.

FARMING — The batsman is said to farm the strike when he faces more deliveries than his batting partner. Also refers to gardening (see below) and to a batsman repairing any divots on the pitch.

FAST — A bowler who delivers the ball at a high speed.

FAST MEDIUM — A pace bowler whose speed of delivery ranks between fast and medium pace.

FEATHERBED — A pitch that is a batting paradise, with no movement off the seam or spin.

FERRET — A tail-end batsman who has limited ability in batting and scoring runs. The bowler usually dismisses him very quickly.

FETCH — Describes a stroke made by the batsman where he stretches to the off side to pull the ball onto the leg side.

FIELDING POSITIONS — Eleven fielders are on the field of play at any one time. While an over is in progress there is a bowler at one end and the wicket-keeper takes up his position behind the stumps at the other end. The other nine fielders are strategically placed in the field of play, depending on the type of bowler, the type of pitch and the match situation. (See diagram on p. 81.)

FIELDSMAN: *Law 41* — The fieldsman may stop the ball with his hands or any part of his person except his hat; otherwise five runs are added to the total of the batting team. There is a fielding restriction on the leg side behind the square leg umpire of no more than two fieldsmen; otherwise the umpire will call 'No ball'. No fieldsman other than the bowler is allowed on the pitch while a ball is being bowled. A batsman cannot be caught off a fieldsman's helmet. When a fieldsman doesn't require his helmet, it is placed behind the wicket-keeper. If the ball hits the helmet, five runs are added to the batting team's score.

FIERY — A bowler who can bowl at an express pace. Also refers to a pitch that assists the bowler when the ball will lift sharply.

FINGER-SPIN — A method used by a slow bowler, who imparts spin to the ball by using his fingers.

FIRST-CLASS COUNTY CRICKET — This type of cricket is played in England between the major playing counties: Derbyshire, Durham, Essex, Glamorgan, Gloucestershire, Hampshire, Kent, Lancashire, Leicestershire, Middlesex, Northamptonshire, Nottinghamshire, Somerset, Surrey, Sussex, Warwickshire, Worcestershire and Yorkshire.

The teams must comprise 11 players and the game is played over a minimum of three days. The local authority decides whether the players are of a quality for their cricket to be described as first-class.

FIRST-CLASS MATCH — A match between two teams, each comprising 11 players. The duration of the match is a minimum of three days. The local authority ensures that the quality of play is up to first-class standard.

FITNESS: *Law 3.8* — This law empowers the umpires to decide whether the pitch is fit for play and whether the light and general weather conditions are fair to both sides. The umpires may agree the conditions are not fit for play, but if both captains agree then play will continue. If the captains do not agree, the umpires have the final decision.

FLANNELS — The traditional cream or white clothing worn by cricketers.

FLAT — A wicket that is very easy paced, with a consistent bounce of the ball. A good batting pitch that allows for stroke play. Also refers to a slow bowler's faster delivery that is pushed through the air quickly with a lower trajectory.

FLAT BAT — A rarely executed stroke off a short-pitched delivery that has pitched outside the off stump and is struck back past the bowler, with the bat coming through horizontally above waist height.

FLIGHT — The ability of a bowler (usually a spin bowler) to deceive a batsman about the length of the ball, by making the delivery dip in the air. This confuses the batsman about where the ball may pitch, making him readjust his shot.

FLIPPER — A type of delivery said to be invented by the Australian legspin bowler Clarrie Grimmett. Flippers have also been bowled to good effect by Richie Benaud and, more recently, by Shane Warne. The ball is held in the tips of the first and third fingers of the right hand and squeezed or flipped out of the hand from underneath the wrist. It is pitched on or about the off stump and is bowled much more quickly than the traditional leg-spinner, causing the batsman to hurry his shot. When the ball pitches it goes through straight but sometimes moves off the pitch from the off stump to the leg stump. This type of ball is very effective if a batsman plays off the back foot and attempts the pull shot — the ball can skid through low, sometimes trapping the batsman lbw.

FLOATER — A spinner's delivery, when the ball is imparted with underspin that tends to make the ball carry further down the pitch than the batsman would have expected.

FLOOR — A colloquial term for the pitch or field of play. The field is also sometimes referred to as the carpet.

FLYER — A fast, short-pitched delivery that comes through at head height to the batsman.

FLY SLIP — A fielding position that is only occasionally used. Midway between the slips and the third man position, it is intended to catch out a batsman who cuts or slashes the ball in the air through that area.

FOLLOW ON: *Law 13* — If a side is 200 runs or more behind the team batting first in a five-day match, 150 runs behind in a three- or four-day match, 100 runs behind in a two-day match or 75 runs behind in a one-day match, the opposing captain can invite the batting team to bat again or follow on immediately.

FOLLOW THROUGH — The act of a bowler's arm finishing down the left side of the body for a right-handed bowler after ball release. Also refers to the bowler's run-off after delivering the ball. In batting, it is the flourishing motion after the ball has been struck and the bat ends over the batsman's shoulder.

FORWARD STROKE — A shot played by the batsman when he advances his front foot towards the pitch of the ball.

POUR RUNS — Runs scored by the batsman when he hits the ball along the ground over the boundary line.

FRENCH CUT — An unintentional shot played by the batsman which is a thick inside edge off the bat that narrowly misses the leg stump. The ball goes towards the fine leg position, usually for some runs. This is not a shot that batsmen practise or want to play because some of the thick inside edges hit the stumps and the batsman is out bowled.

FRISKY or FIERY PITCH — A pitch that has too much moisture in it or too much grass, or a pitch that is too dry so that the ball jumps awkwardly. Life for the batsman is difficult because the bowler has all the advantages, with the ball seaming and bouncing off a length.

FRONT ON — In bowling, when the bowler is square-chested, rather than side on to the batsman at delivery. This makes it difficult for the bowler to swing the ball because there is less body action.

In batting, the batsman faces the ball, rather than being in a side-on position when the bowler delivers the ball. This normally means the batsman will hit across the line of the ball and hit it on the leg side.

FULL-BLOODED — In batting, a stroke played with full power.

FULL TOSS, FULL PEE, FULL BUNGER or **FULL-PITCHED** — A ball that reaches the batsman at the popping crease without pitching, or a ball that the batsman makes into a full toss by advancing down the pitch and hitting before it has landed.

FURNITURE — A colloquial term used for the stumps. A commentator may say 'the batsman has had his furniture removed' (the batsman has been clean bowled).

GARDENING — When a batsman walks down the pitch to brush aside any debris and tap down any divots so that the ball will not hit them and create batting problems.

GATE — The attendance or takings at the turnstiles for a day's play or during a match. 'Through the gate' is the term used when the ball passes between the batsman's bat and pad.

GAUGE — Instrument used by the umpire to measure the width of a bat and the circumference of the ball to ensure the laws of the game are not transgressed.

GAUNTLETS — A manufacturer's term for wicket-keeping gloves.

GENTLEMEN — An old term used to describe amateur players. In the early days matches were played between the Gentlemen and the Players.

GIVE THE BALL SOME AIR — Refers to a spin bowler tossing the ball further into the air, allowing it drop.

GLANCE — A shot played by the batsman in which the ball is deflected off the bat down the leg side.

GLOVEMAN — Another term for the wicket-keeper. 'He's a good gloveman' means the wicket-keeper is very efficient behind the stumps.

GLOVE, TO THE KEEPER — Colloquial term used when the ball has hit the batsman's glove and is caught by the wicket-keeper.

GLUEPOT — Refers to a sticky or drying wicket.

GOING AWAY — A ball bowled by the bowler that leaves the bat either in the air or off the seam.

GOING WITH THE ARM — A term that is used for a ball that appears to go with the direction of the arm, i.e. for a right-arm bowler it is the continuation of an outswinger, and for a left-arm bowler the continuation of an inswinger.

GOLDEN DUCK — The batsman has been dismissed first ball without scoring. A golden pair is being dismissed first ball in each innings.

GOOD EYE — The ability of a batsman to assess the nature of a delivery and move quickly into position and play the correct stroke.

GOOD LENGTH — A ball pitched by the bowler which causes the batsman to be uncertain about whether he should play back or forward. On most pitches, a good length is about 3 metres in front of the batsman, but this will vary according to the pitch conditions.

GOOGLY — A ball that is bowled out of the back of a hand from a right arm leg-spinner. It looks like a leg-spinner but, when the ball pitches, it spins back towards the batsman as an off-break. If the batsman is unable to recognise this type of delivery, he can be deceived. This type of ball is also called a wrong 'un because it spins the wrong way, or a Bosie.

'GO-SUNDER' — Slang term used for a ball that stays low and causes the batsman problems. From 'goes under the bat'.

GRAFTER — A batsman who is prepared to occupy the crease for long periods of time, taking few risks in collecting runs through singles and twos. Generally, such a player has a sound batting technique and can concentrate for long periods of time.

GRASSY PITCH — A pitch where the grass has not been shaved down close to the ground. Such a wicket assists the seam bowler because the ball grips the grass, causing it to deviate.

GREASY — A rain-affected pitch is said to be greasy.

GREEN WICKET or **PITCH** — A well-grassed pitch on which the faster bowlers usually prosper because the ball will move or seam off the pitch. It is often referred to as a 'green-top' and is a pitch that bowlers enjoy and batsmen fear.

GRIP — Under certain pitch conditions, the ball will grip by either seaming or bouncing quite sharply off the pitch.

GROUND FIELDING — The part of fielding that doesn't include catching.

GROUNDSMAN — The person who prepares the pitch and the playing outfield and ensures that they are fit for play. He will water, cut and roll the pitch and cut the outfield. Also called a curator.

GRUBBER — A ball that stays very low after hitting the pitch.

GUARD — When the batsman arrives at the crease he will ask the umpire for a guard. The umpire will indicate to him, usually from over the stumps the line to his middle, middle and leg or leg stump. There the batsman will make his mark or block hole and that is where he will ground his bat when he takes strike to face the bowler. The batsman should know the exact position of his stumps in relation to where he stands.

GULLY — A fielding position between the slips and the point area close to the wicket on the off side, usually 15 metres from the bat. The gully will often take catches in that area when a batsman plays a cut shot.

HALF COCK — An improvised stroke from the batsman that is neither forward nor back, leaving him stranded on the crease and vulnerable to dismissal.

HALF VOLLEY — A ball that is pitched well up to the batsman so that, as he moves forward, the bat and the front foot are close to the ball. It is usually hit for runs, sometimes four. Batsmen enjoy facing such deliveries.

HANDLED THE BALL: *Law 33* — Either batsman can be given out handled ball if he touches the ball, while in play, with his hand, unless doing so with the approval of the fielding team.

HARROW — A bat just short of the full size, which is well suited to a young player or a very short adult.

HAT TRICK — A bowler is credited with this rare achievement if he dismisses three batsmen with consecutive deliveries during one over or spread over two overs. By long-standing custom, it will also be a hat trick if the three consecutive balls are spread over two innings.

HELMET — This has now become an essential part of a batsman's protective equipment. In 1977 England's Mike Brearley developed and wore a fibreglass skull cap that fitted under his cap. The helmet evolved from World Series Cricket and has a visor attached to the front and/or side guards to protect the temple area. Close-in fielders also wear helmets.

HIT THE BALL TWICE: *Law 34* — A batsman is out if he hits the ball twice, unless the stroke is made in defence of his wicket, i.e. stopping the ball from hitting the wickets. No runs can be scored off the second stroke except from an overthrow. The bowler does not get the credit of the wicket if the batsman is given out hit the ball twice.

HIT WICKET: *Law 35* — A batsman is out hit wicket if he hits the wicket with his bat or any part of his person. This includes his cap falling onto the stumps and the bails falling off during the course of playing a shot at the ball.

HOLD ONE BACK — In an attempt to deceive the batsman, the bowler releases the ball before the hand reaches the top of its delivery arc. The ball will take a fraction longer to reach the batsman and a mistimed shot may result.

HOOKER — Describes a batsman who produces a spectacular leg-side shot to short-pitched and rising deliveries from a bowler, resulting in a six, four or sometimes his dismissal when he is caught near the boundary.

HOOK SHOT — A stroke made to a short rising ball, usually pitching on leg stump, which is hit on the leg side behind or just in front of square leg.

HOW'S THAT? HOWZAT! — An appeal made by the fielding team to the umpire, usually by the bowler and/or the wicket-keeper when they believe the batsman is out.

ICC — The International Cricket Council, which administers the game. The ICC involves representatives of the test-playing countries and the associate countries.

IN — The time from a batsman reaching the crease to start his innings until he is dismissed.

INCOMMODING THE STRIKER: *Law 42.6* — An umpire is justified in calling 'Dead ball' if, in his opinion, a batsman is distracted or incommoded by the fielding team while taking strike against the bowler, i.e. by any noise or action that will disturb his concentration.

INDOOR CRICKET — A form of cricket played indoors and within a net by two teams of limited numbers in a restricted space, and with special rules. A popular recreation for business houses and companies.

INFIELD — Refers to the close-in part-way fieldsmen, as distinct from those in the outfield. The slips, gully, point, cover, mid-off, mid-on, mid-wicket, square leg, leg gully, leg slip and the silly mid-on and silly mid-off positions are considered to be the infield.

INNERS — Soft, close-fitting gloves, made of cotton or chamois, used by a wicket-keeper inside his leather gloves.

INNINGS: *Law 12*—A match will consist of one or two innings per team, depending on the agreement reached before the start of play. All test and first-class matches consist of two innings. In a two-innings match, each team will take their innings alternatively. An innings will last until the batting team has lost 10 wickets or the batting captain declares his team's innings closed. The toss of a coin will decide who will bat first; the winning captain decides whether to bat first or ask the opposition to bat first.

INSIDE EDGE — An involuntary stroke from a batsman, where the ball glances off the inside edge of the bat (the edge of the bat closest to the pad) and sometimes goes down to the fine leg fieldsman for runs.

INSLANT — Bowling, usually directed from wide or from the edge of the crease, by a right-arm over the wicket bowler and directed at, or even outside, the leg stump. This is regarded as negative bowling and in one-day matches any balls that pitch outside the leg stump will be called wide by the umpire.

INSWINGER — A ball that swings or curves in the air from about the off stump to the leg stump in flight and moves in towards the batsman.

INTERNATIONAL CODE OF CONDUCT: *Law 42.13* — The ICC has appointed match referees to be present at all international matches to enforce the Code of Conduct. This relates to fair play, intimidation, player abuse, over rates and any other action that could bring the game into disrepute. (See Chapter 9.)

INTERROGATION — The bowler is said to interrogate the batsman by pitching the ball in a certain place to see how he will play the ball. Most bowlers will interrogate the batsman by probing the off-stump area.

INTERVALS — These refer to breaks in play such as 40 minutes for lunch and 20 minutes for afternoon tea.

INTERVENTION BY THE UMPIRES: *Law 42.3* — The umpires are allowed to intervene and stop play by calling dead ball if they consider that an aspect of play is unfair, e.g. persistent short-pitched bowling, sledging, etc. Otherwise they should not interfere with the progress of play except as required by the law.

INTIMIDATION: *Law 42.8* — Allows the umpire to decide whether the bowling of fast, short-pitched deliveries is fair or unfair. If the umpire feels that too many bouncers or bumpers are being bowled to intimidate the batsman or that the bowler is deliberately trying to hit or injure the batsman, he can warn the bowler. If the bowler continues, he will receive a second warning and the captain is advised. If he still persists, the umpire can remove the bowler from the crease for the rest of that innings.

JAFFER — A colloquial term for an unplayable ball or the perfect delivery that unsettles and sometimes dismisses the batsman.

JAG — A colloquial term for a ball that cuts or seams off the pitch.

JUMBO — A type of bat developed with extra wood and thick edges. It is heavier than the more conventional bat and offers the batsman more power if the ball is struck firmly.

KING PAIR — When the batsman has been dismissed first ball in each innings of the match without scoring. This would be regarded as the ultimate batting nightmare.

KNOCK — Another word for an individual innings. A commentator may say, for example, 'That was a fine knock of 120.' Sometimes the batsman will knock or work in his new bat by using a ball mallet.

LAP SHOT — This is dressing-room slang for a cross-bat shot that carts the ball in front of or just behind square leg. Generally known as the sweep shot.

LAST OVER — This is the final over of a bowler's spell, before an interval, or the final over of the day's play. Usually, however, it applies to the final over on the last day of a match and will be completed at the request of either captain, even if a wicket has fallen.

LATE CUT — A stroke played by the batsman to a short ball that has pitched outside the off stump and when the batsman steps back and across the stumps and hits down and over the top of the ball with a wristy action, sending the ball past the slips area. This shot is usually played against a spin bowler or a medium pace bowler.

LAWS OF CRICKET — These 42 laws relate to the way the game is played — the pitch and oval dimensions, how a batsman can be dismissed, special requirements relating to the ball and bat, declarations, unfair play, appeals, fitness of the playing conditions, the spirit in which the game should be played and other aspects in the game. The laws should not be confused with rules, which apply only to special conditions such as the start and finish times and other aspects relating to a match.

LEFT-ARM ORTHODOX SPIN BOWLER — A left-arm finger-spinner who bowls a ball pitching on or about the middle stump, turning or spinning the ball from leg to off or from right to left.

LEG BEFORE WICKET (LBW): *Law 36* — A batsman can be dismissed lbw if the ball hits the batsman or any part of his body excluding the bat and there is an appeal from the fielding team. The umpire must decide several things before he gives the batsman out:

- Would the ball have hit the wickets?
- Did the ball pitch on a straight line between one set of wickets and the other set of wickets?
- Did the ball pitch on the off side of the wicket but hit the batsman (usually on the pads) in line with the set of wickets at each end?
- Did the batsman deliberately pad up to a ball pitched outside the off stump and offer no genuine shot at the ball, which would have carried on and hit the wickets?

This is the most controversial dismissal decision the umpire has to make because the margin of error is so small. Some batsmen can feel hard done by because they got a little bat or inside edge on the ball before the ball hit the pads. (See diagram on p. 102.) A batsman cannot be given out lbw if the ball has pitched outside the leg stump.

LEG-BREAK — A ball that turns or spins off the pitch from the leg side to the offside. The right-arm wrist leg-spinner and the left-arm orthodox spin bowler bowl these balls to a right-handed batsman.

LEG BYES: *Law 26* — These are scored when the ball is unintentionally deflected off the batsman's person when he is attempting to play at the ball. The ball normally comes off the pads, the thighpad and, on rare occasions, off the batsman's head or helmet. For runs to be scored, the umpire must decide that the batsman has played a genuine shot at the ball, including taking evasive action. If he has not played a genuine shot, the umpire will call 'Dead ball'.

LEG-CUTTER — A fast leg break bowled by cutting the fingers across and down the left-hand side of the ball, causing it to rotate in the air. When the ball hits the pitch, it grips and moves off the seam from the leg side to the off side.

LEG SIDE — The side of the field that is behind the batsman as he takes his stance or guard at the wicket. His legs are on that side of the wicket, hence leg side.

LEG THEORY — A method of bowling that is frowned upon because it is negative and not in the best interests or the spirit of the game. The ball is consistently pitched on or just outside the leg stump, with most of the fielders positioned on the leg side to prevent the batsman scoring runs. The fielders are known as the leg trap.

LEG TRAP — A ring of close-in fielders positioned on the leg side to an inslant/inswing bowler or a fast bowler who is directing the ball at the batsman's upper body. The field is set in the hope of a batsman offering a fielder a catch. The field is also set for an off-spin bowler.

LENGTH — This is the point at which the ball lands on the pitch when delivered by the bowler.

LIFTING THE SEAM: *Law 42.4* — A fielder or bowler is not allowed to lift the seam of the ball. If the umpire finds that a ball has been tampered with, he can change it for one that is in similar condition to the original ball before the offence took place.

LIGHT — The degree of light visible to allow play to continue so that the batsman is not disadvantaged. The fitness of the light before the start of play is in the hands of the umpires. Once play has started, the batsmen will be allowed one light appeal per session. If the umpires consider the light to be bad and that there is a chance of injury to the batsmen or that they are placed at a disadvantage, play is suspended until the light improves. The fielding side cannot appeal against the light.

LIGHT METER — A device used by the umpires to determine whether the light is good enough for safe and fair play.

LOB — A method of bowling that is not seen much these days. The lob can be a ball that is bowled underarm but in most forms of cricket this has been banned. Youngsters, however, tend to bowl this way in their early development. The lob is also a donkey drop, where the ball is lobbed into the air with the intention that it should land behind the batsman and hit the wickets on the full.

LOFTED — A ball hit in the air by the batsman, usually clearing the infield.

LOLLY — A colloquial term for a simple catch.

LONG FIELD — Another term for the fielders positioned in the outfield, e.g. third man, fine leg, deep mid-on, deep mid-off, deep square leg and the sweepers positioned close to the boundary. (See the diagrams in Chapter 5.)

LONG HANDLE — A colloquial term for a batsman throwing caution to the wind and playing some adventurous shots.

LONG HOP — A ball short enough to be safely pulled off the back foot by the batsman to the on side.

LONG LEG — This is a fielding position near the boundary on the leg side behind the wicket, midway between fine leg and square leg.

LONG OFF — A fielding position behind the bowler near the boundary edge on the off side. A deeper position than mid-off.

LONG ON — This is a fielding position behind the bowler on the leg side near the boundary. A deeper position than mid-on.

LONG STOP — This term usually applies in youngsters' games of cricket. A fielder is positioned behind the wicket-keeper near the boundary as a back-up in case the keeper misses the ball.

LOST BALL: *Law 20*—If a ball is lost in the field of play, the fielding team may call lost ball and six runs are added to the batting team's score. If, however, more than six runs have been scored before lost ball has been called, the runs scored will count. Lost balls on the field of play are very rare; on some grounds, balls have disappeared down rabbit holes.

LUNCH INTERVAL — This break (usually 40 minutes) happens most commonly two hours after the start of play in first-class matches, unless special conditions apply. The lunch break may also be adjusted according to the weather conditions. In test matches, play is in two-hour sessions.

MAIDEN OVER — An over in which no runs are scored off the bat. If a wicket falls in the course of an over and still no runs are scored off the bat, a wicket maiden is bowled.

MANAGER — Most first-class teams and certainly test teams have a manager, who is usually responsible for all the administrative matters associated with the efficient running of the team. He or she will be in charge of accommodation, travel arrangements, paying the bills, team discipline, team harmony and making sure that team meetings are orderly. The manager reports and makes recommendations in writing to the local cricket authority on all aspects of the team during the season, including any tours that have been undertaken.

MAN IN — A call, usually made by the captain of the fielding team, saying that the new batsman has arrived at the crease and the fielders should return to their fielding positions.

MANKAD — A colloquial term used for the act of running a batsman out at the non-striker's end by the bowler before the ball has been released. It is named after India's Vinoo Mankad, who ran a batsman out in this manner. It is generally held that a bowler should first warn a batsman if he is backing up too early and leaving his ground.

MATCH REFEREE — Appointed by the ICC to be present at all international matches to enforce the Code of Conduct. He or she is a neutral referee, i.e. comes from a different country than either of the two teams who are playing. (See Chapter 9.)

MATTING PITCH — A form of artificial strip wicket, made of hemp when a proper grass pitch cannot be laid. The matting is usually laid over concrete or a clay base. In some countries and in some conditions, the matting pitch favours the wrist-spin bowlers because they push the ball through quickly and the ball fizzes and bounces awkwardly off the matting. It has been said that, in some countries, the matting pitch was stretched or loosened depending on whether the local team batted or bowled first, to give them an unfair advantage.

MAXIMUM — Term used by players and commentators for a batsman hitting a six, which is the maximum runs that can be hit from one ball.

MCC — The Marylebone Cricket Club is a private club formed in 1787. Accepted as the law-making body of the game, it owns Lord's Cricket Ground in London. Lord's is regarded as the home of cricket, full of tradition and history and holder of the famous Ashes urn. The MCC promotes the game, its ethics of fair play and sportsmanship, and has an exclusive membership. Women were admitted for the first time in 1998.

MEAT — Refers to the middle of the bat, which is the thickest part. The power in the bat comes from this area.

MIDDLE — Refers to the wicket area, the place where all the action is happening in the game. Also refers to the sweet spot in the middle of the bat and the guard taken by the batsman in line from one middle stump to the other middle stump.

MISFIELD — A misfield occurs when a fielder attempts to stop the ball and misses it, sometimes resulting in additional runs for the batsman. Misfields often occur when the fielder has no part of his body as a second line of defence when attempting to stop the ball with his hands. Lapses in concentration, poor technique and the use of one hand instead of two are causes of misfields.

MISHIT — A mistimed or misplaced stroke by a batsman due to bad timing, poor body positioning, poor shot selection or a lapse in concentration. Also called a miscue.

MOVEMENT — This usually relates to how much sideways deviation a bowler can get on the ball either in the air or off the pitch. Movement relates to swing in the air or seam or cut off the pitch.

NECK AND CROP — A batsman is beaten all ends up. He has played at and missed the ball.

NET BOWLER — A bowler who is asked to come to a practice and bowl to the specialist batsmen in the nets while the regular first team bowlers are rested. They are asked to do the donkey work, especially a day or two before an important match, so that the main bowlers remain fresh for that game. This is also an opportunity for the net bowler to impress the selectors.

NETS — A place where a team will practise batting and bowling skills before a match begins. The practice pitch is surrounded by a net to prevent the ball from being hit away.

NEW BALL: *Law 5.3* — Either captain may demand a new ball at the start of each innings. The captain also has the option of taking a second new ball after a certain number of overs have been completed with the old ball, usually after 80 overs in first-class matches unless special conditions allow for it to be taken earlier.

The new ball is very hard, it has a raised seam and it swings more in the air than an older ball. The faster bowlers prefer using the new ball because it gives them an advantage.

NIGHT CRICKET — This evolved out of Kerry Packer's World Series Cricket in 1977. The lights went on and the cricketing world has enjoyed the excitement of day-night cricket ever since. The white ball, black sight-screens and coloured clothing have captured the imagination of many enthusiasts and the players appear to enjoy playing these games. Matches usually start at 2.30 p.m. and finish at 10.15 p.m.

NIGHT-WATCHMAN — A lower order batsman who is promoted in the batting order in the place of a recognised batsman. This sometimes occurs 20 minutes before the end of play. His job is to stay out there until the end of the day's play and, where possible, to protect the other batsman from taking the strike. If the nightwatchman does his job successfully, he will continue his innings the next day. Some lower order batsmen relish the job because it gives them the opportunity to prove that they can score runs and accept responsibility.

NO BALL: *Law 24* — There are six different infringements where an umpire can call 'No ball':

➤ The bowler has thrown the ball at delivery instead of bowling it.

➤ The bowler's front foot has landed in front of the batting or popping crease at the point of ball release,

➤ The bowler's back foot has touched the return crease or forward extension at the point of ball release,

➤ The bowler has not advised the batsman via the umpire that he intends to change his delivery from over the wicket to around the wicket or that he intends to bowl with the opposite arm from the previous delivery,

➤ There are more than two fielders positioned behind square on the leg side at the point of delivery,

➤ In a one-day match, a ball delivered above the waist is also a no ball.

The ball is still alive on the call of 'no ball' because runs can be scored and the batsman can be dismissed in one of four ways: run out, handled the ball, obstructing the field and hit the ball twice. If a no ball has been called, the batting team will automatically benefit by at least one run and the ball has to be rebowled. See the diagrams opposite.

NON-STRIKER — The batsman who is not receiving the ball and is positioned at the umpire's end while the bowler delivers the ball to the striker at the other end. If the striker scores a single or there is one leg bye or one bye, the non-striker will then become the striker and face the next delivery from the bowler.

NOT CRICKET — A phrase used when a set of circumstances or actions taken is not acceptable in the code of behaviour. The spirit and ethics of the game may have been breached.

NOTHING BALL — A bowled ball that does very little in the air or off the pitch. It is bowled at medium pace or by a spinner and doesn't cause the batsman any problems.

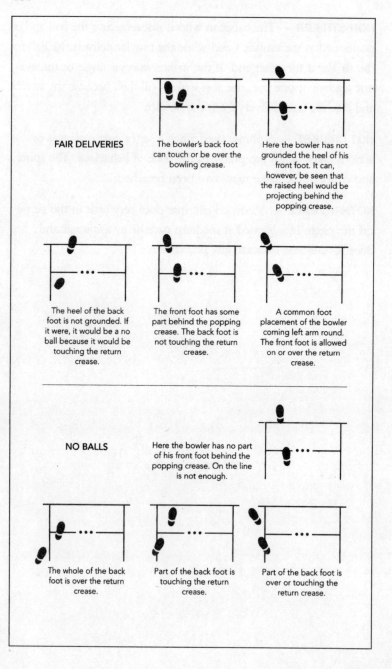

NOT OUT—If the team's innings ends, the batsman who has not been dismissed is left not out. If there is a declaration, then both batsmen are left not out.

NZC INC. — New Zealand Cricket Incorporated. Used to be known as NZCC, the New Zealand Cricket Council, and administers the game of cricket in New Zealand.

OBSTRUCTING THE FIELD: *Law 37* — Either batsman can be out obstructing the field if, on appeal and in the opinion of the umpire, he has wilfully obstructed the opposition by word or action, e.g. preventing a fieldsman from taking a catch or yelling out.

OBSTRUCTION OF THE BATSMAN WHEN RUNNING: *Law 42.7* — It is considered unfair play if the fielding team wilfully obstructs the batsman while he is running between the wickets. The umpire will call 'Dead ball' if he considers the batsman to be impeded and the batsman will benefit from the runs he has scored before the obstruction.

OFF-BREAK or **OFF-SPIN** — Bowled by the off-spin bowler, who spins the ball mainly with the first finger of the right hand with an action similar to opening a door handle. The ball pitches around the off-stump area and spins back towards the batsman to the leg side.

OFF-CUTTER — A type of delivery that in effect is a fast off-break, with the fingers of a right-hand bowler being dragged across the seam and pulled down the right side of the ball. When the ball hits the pitch it moves from the off side to the leg side.

OFF-DRIVE — A forceful stroke played by the batsman off the front foot, with a vertical bat hitting the ball between the cover and mid-off fielding positions.

OFF SIDE — The side of the field the batsman faces when he takes strike. The positions include the slips, gully, third man, point, cover and mid-off.

OLD BALL — A ball that has been used for some time in an innings. Spin bowlers generally prefer to bowl with the older ball because it is easier to grip.

ON-DRIVE — A forceful stroke played by the batsman from the front foot with a vertical bat hitting the ball on the on side towards mid-on to mid-wicket.

ONE-DAY CRICKET — Each team bats for a limited number of overs agreed upon by both teams, e.g. 50 overs. A result is achieved on that day and the winner is the team that scores the most runs. This is irrespective of the number of wickets that have been lost by either team. Bowlers usually have a limitation on the number of overs they are permitted to bowl, generally no more than 10. Fielding restrictions apply.

ONE-DAY INTERNATIONAL (ODI) — A one-day match between two countries with two teams of II players.

ONE SHORT — A batsman is deemed to have taken a short run if he fails to ground his bat over the batting crease when attempting more than one run. The umpire will signal to the scorers and that run is not counted.

ON SIDE — The same as the leg side or the side of the field behind the batsman. The positions include fine leg, square leg, leg gully, silly mid-on (bat-pad), short leg, mid-wicket and mid-on.

OUT CRICKET — The operations of the fielding team in relation to bowling, wicket-keeping and fielding skills.

OUTER — The area from which spectators view the match.

OUTFIELD — The portion of the playing area where the fielding positions are nearer the boundary than the pitch; it includes long off, long on, deep third man, fine leg, deep mid-wicket and long leg.

OUT OF HIS GROUND: *Law 29* — The batsman must have some part of his foot or bat grounded behind the batting or popping crease to avoid being stumped by the wicket-keeper or run out by him or the fieldsman. If the foot or bat is placed on the line, the batsman is out.

OUTSIDE EDGE — An involuntary stroke played by the batsman with the ball hitting the outside edge of the bat, sometimes resulting in runs with the ball going down to third man, or the batsman being caught by the wicket-keeper or in the slips/gully area.

OUTSWINGER — A ball that swings in the air and leaves the right-handed batsman moving away to outside the off stump towards the slips.

OVER: *Law 22* — An over comprises six fair deliveries bowled from one end of the pitch or wicket. After the sixth ball has been bowled the umpire will call 'Over' or 'Over bowled'. Consecutive overs are bowled from alternate ends of the pitch, by different bowlers. In test cricket, a minimum of 90 overs must be bowled in a day's play.

In 1744 four-ball overs were bowled in England, increased to five balls in 1899 and six balls in 1900. In 1939 an eight-ball over was introduced as a trial but was not continued after the war.

In Australia four-ball overs increased to six in 1887. In 1918 Australia adopted the eight-ball over, retaining it until 1980 when they reverted to the six-ball over.

In a first-class match, it would be normal for the batting team to score between 250 and 320 in 90 overs or a day's play, depending on conditions.

OVERHEAD CONDITIONS — Relates to the weather conditions, which can have a dramatic effect on the game. Hot and humid conditions allow the ball to move or swing more in the air. A breeze will also assist movement in the air and give the bowler an advantage. Cool, wet conditions will keep any moisture in the pitch for a longer period of time, helping the seam bowler to get cut off the wicket. Hot, dry conditions will take any moisture out of the pitch and allow for a very good batting pitch on which batsmen may prosper. Such conditions will also allow a dry pitch to wear and crumble, allowing a spin bowler to prosper.

OVERSPIN — Commonly called top spin. The top of the ball is rotating forward and the bottom of the ball is rotating backwards.

OVER THE WICKET — Bowling over the wicket is when the bowler's arm delivering the ball is the arm closer to the wickets or stumps.

OVERTHROWS — Runs accruing to the batsman or the batting team when the ball from the outfield is returned and eludes the wicket-keeper or the fielder guarding the stumps at the bowler's end.

PACE — All modes of bowling except spin, from medium-paced to very fast. Also refers to the pace of the pitch — whether it is fast, slow or medium paced, i.e. the pace at which the ball comes off the pitch.

PACEMAN — Refers to any bowler who delivers the ball at high speed.

PADS — Protective equipment worn by the batsman, which includes leg guards, thighpads, an arm guard and a chest protector. The wicket-keeper will also wear a pair of pads, gloves and, on rare occasions, a chest protector.

PAD UP — The batsman has pushed forward to a ball that has usually pitched well outside the off stump and instead of using his bat, he allows the ball to hit his pads. If the batsman misjudges the line of the ball and if, in the opinion of the umpire, the ball would have carried on and hit the stumps, the batsman will be out lbw.

Also refers to a batsman preparing for his innings by putting on his pads.

PAIR OF SPECTACLES — Something that a batsman is never proud of and tries to avoid: scoring no runs or two ducks in the same match. The two noughts look like a pair of spectacles.

PARTNERSHIPS — When two batsmen bat together they form a batting partnership, and the total runs scored between them, including any extras, are attributed to that 'partnership'. This terminates at the dismissal of either batsman, and a new partnership begins with the incoming batsman.

PAVILION — The central point of any cricket ground. The players will have their changing and eating facilities in the pavilion. Members will view the match from the pavilion and enjoy any special privileges offered by the club. Some spectators may be fortunate in having a seat in the main stand or pavilion area. Some pavilions display the club's history, with memorabilia such as photographs, old bats, ties, balls and clothes worn by former players.

PICK — In batting this refers to assessing a bowler's delivery. In bowling, it is the illegal practice of lifting the seam of the ball to give the bowler an unfair advantage.

PICKETS — Colloquial term for the boundary, as some boundary lines at first-class venues have a picket fence, hence the term 'the ball has hit the pickets'.

PINCH HITTER — Usually a lower order batsman promoted in the order with a specific instruction to change the course of a game by scoring quick runs or hitting a respected bowler out of the attack. He usually has the captain's approval to take risks in trying to hit sixes and fours. This can be very exciting and entertaining if the batsman is enjoying some success. More often than not, these innings are very brief with a batsman contributing a quickfire 20 or 30.

PITCH/WICKET: *Law 7* — The area between the two creases and where the ball will eventually land. It measures 1.52 metres (5 feet) in width on either side of the line joining the centre of the middle stumps of the wickets. The total length of the pitch, including the bowling and batting creases, is 20.12 metres (22 yards). The pitch has to be prepared before the toss of the coin and it is up to the local authority to ensure that the pitch is up to standard. Once the match is in progress, the umpires are in control to ensure the pitch is not damaged by the players. The pitch cannot be changed during the course of a match unless it becomes unfit for play and, even then, both captains must agree. The pitch can be rolled, swept and remarked at designated times. (See diagram on p. 77.)

PITCHED — Where the ball has landed or pitched on the pitch or wicket when released by the bowler.

PLAY AND MISS — When the batsman plays a genuine shot at the ball but fails to make contact.

PLAY AT — The batsman offers a stroke at the ball, whether he makes contact or not.

PLAYED ON — A ball that has hit the bat or part of the batsman's body and rolled onto the stumps, dislodging the bail or bails. It is entered in the scorebook as bowled.

PLAYERS: *Law 1* — A match is played between two teams each of 11 players. Each team will have a captain and, if the captain is unavailable, a deputy or vice-captain will be appointed. Before the toss of a coin, the captain must declare his playing team to the opposing captain. Other forms of cricket have more or less than 11 players, but no more than 11 players can take the field at any one time.

PLAYERS DAMAGING THE PITCH: *Law 42.11*— The umpires are responsible for ensuring that the players do not wilfully or unintentionally damage the pitch. The batsmen are not allowed to run down the middle of the pitch while attempting to score a run and bowlers in their follow through must stay out of the danger area. The umpire will give the bowler or the batsmen a caution, followed by a final warning, and then report players if they keep infringing. A bowler can be removed from the bowling crease for the rest of the innings if he keeps running into the danger area.

PLAYING BACK — A shot played by the batsman when his body weight is transferred to the back foot, which therefore moves towards the stumps so that he plays the ball off the back foot. This shot is played to a ball that has pitched short of a length.

PLAYING BLOCK — The area where all the pitches are prepared for playing a match. Some playing blocks may have an area where 10 or more pitches can be used during the season.

PLAYING FORWARD — A stroke offered by the batsman when he pushes his front leg up the pitch towards the ball. This type of shot is played to a ball that has been well pitched up or when the pitch is low and slow and the batsman is trying to avoid a possible lbw decision.

PLUMB LBW — The batsman has played back to a ball that has kept low and he has been hit on the pads in front of the stumps. This will result in an appeal from the fielding team, usually the bowler and the wicket-keeper, and the umpire will give the batsman out lbw.

PLUMB PITCH — A perfect pitch that has not been affected by the weather or deteriorated in any way while the match is in progress. It gives no help to the faster bowlers or the spin bowlers, with the ball coming off the pitch at good pace and at a consistent and regular height. These conditions are ideal for batting.

POINT — A fielding position close to the wicket square on the off side about 20 metres from the batsman.

POPPING CREASE: *Law 9* — A line 1.2 metres (4 feet) in front of the wicket parallel to the bowling crease. This is the line where the batsman has safety and cannot be stumped or run out, provided he has part of his foot or the bat grounded behind the line. He will also mark his guard or block hole on that line. The bowler must also have his front foot grounded behind the line at the point of delivery otherwise the umpire will call 'no ball'. (See diagram on p. 76.)

PROFESSIONAL — A player or coach who makes their living by being contracted to their county, province, state or country. They receive a salary or fee for their services and some players will share in match bonuses and incentive schemes. Also refers to the attitude of a player.

PROTECTOR — Another term for the 'box' or abdominal protector which protects the genitals of a batsman, wicket-keeper or close-in fieldsman.

PULL OUT — A colloquial term for a captain declaring the innings closed and allowing the opposition to bat. Also refers to a batsman getting into a position to play a stroke then changing his mind and stopping the shot.

PULL SHOT — A stroke made by hitting across the flight of the ball which has pitched on or outside the off stump and is pulled to the on side, usually in front of square leg. It is usually played off the front foot and hit downwards.

PUT IN — Having won the toss, the captain has told the opposition to bat first. This usually happens when the pitch offers assistance to the faster bowlers and the captain is seeking an early advantage in the match. In bowling, it means to provide extra effort.

PUT ON — In bowling, a bowler brought on to bowl; in batting, two batsmen scoring runs in a partnership, i.e. 'to put on runs'.

PUT THE SHUTTERS UP — The batting team has decided that they cannot win the match so they play cautiously and very defensively in an attempt not to lose any wickets. They play many dead bat shots.

QUICK — A colloquial term for a fast bowler or the pace of a bowler.

QUICKIE — A slang term for a fast bowler.

QUICK PITCH/WICKET — A hard pitch that allows the ball to come off quickly. This type of pitch is usually produced by a lot of rolling with a heavy roller. It encourages the faster bowlers but also allows the batsmen to play shots. Sometimes regarded as a perfect pitch, provided the pace and bounce of the ball is consistent.

QUICK RUNS — Taken by the batsmen who decide they can get to the end of the wicket before the fielder can retrieve and return the ball. Also a term used for a team scoring runs quickly so that a declaration or a win can be achieved.

RABBIT — A tail-end batsman who struggles with the finer technical aspects of batting and scores few runs. It also relates to a quality batsman who keeps getting out to the same bowler time and time again. The bowler may say, 'That batsman is my bunny or rabbit.'

RAIN — A steady downpour will halt play and have the fielders heading for the pavilion or the dressing room until conditions are dry enough for the match to continue. If light drizzle is falling before the game, play will not start. If the players are on the field and there is light drizzle, play may continue until the umpires decide it is too wet and conditions are not fair and equal for both teams.

REACH — A batsman's ability to stretch forward from the crease to play a stroke. A taller player with longer legs will have a greater ability to reach forward than a shorter player with short legs. If a batsman has a long reach, it will be more difficult for a spin bowler to find his length.

RECALLING THE BATSMAN — The fielding captain can recall the batsman if he feels the latter has received a bad decision from the umpire. This does not happen very often and usually applies to a caught behind decision when the umpire has given the batsman out but the ball may not have carried to the fielder or wicket-keeper.

RECORDS — All details of every match played are recorded and the statistician dutifully updates all the information that has been recorded in the scorebook. These statistics for bowlers and batsmen become important because players' true ability often reflects what they have been able to achieve in the game, i.e. runs scored, wickets captured and their averages. These statistics or records are compared with those of other players in the game, who are then rated against each other accordingly. Each country, province, club or school team will have match records.

REDPATH CUP — A special award to the New Zealand batsman who has achieved the most meritorious batting performances in first-class cricket matches since the award was last made.

REPORT — A written analysis by the captains of the playing conditions and the standard of umpiring during the match. Also, a written complaint by one or both umpires, the match referee or the opposing team, about a breach in the code of behaviour.

RESULT: *Law 21* — There are several different results in cricket. In a two-innings match, the team that scores more runs in its two completed innings is the winner. A match is drawn if the team batting second fails to reach the runs required and still has at least one wicket intact when scheduled play is finished. A match can be tied when the team batting second loses its last wicket and the scores are equal. In a one-day match, the team that scores more runs, irrespective of wickets lost, is the winner. The umpires can also award the match to a team if the opposition refuses to play or turn up.

RETIRED — When a player has decided to end his cricketing career.

RETIREMENTS: *Law 2.9* — A batsman may retire at any time but cannot resume his innings without the consent of the fielding captain and then only at the fall of a wicket. A batsman is regarded as not out if he retires as a result of injury or illness, but he is out if he retires for any other reason.

RETURN — The throw back to the stumps or at the bowler's end after the ball has been fielded.

RETURN CATCH — The batsman has hit the ball in the air back to the bowler, who has held onto the catch, and the batsman is out caught and bowled.

RETURN CREASE: Law 9 — The line, usually 2.43 metres (8 feet) in length, that comes back at right angles at each end of the bowling crease. This line can be unlimited in length but it is usually extended a metre or so behind the stumps because the back foot no ball law comes into play if the bowler's back foot cuts the return crease line at the point of ball release. (See diagram on p. 76.)

REVERSE SWEEP — A stroke played by the batsman to a spin bowler. The batsman will reverse his grip on the bat as the bowler runs in to bowl and will sweep the ball on the off side of the wicket, usually behind point.

REVERSE SWING — The sideways deviation of the ball while travelling in the air. The ball needs to reach a certain speed and it is usually a ball that is between 40 and 50 overs old. The major roughness of one side of the ball, which results from some furriness of the leather, and the minor roughness of the other side makes the ball swing very sharply and often late. Moisture is generally added to one side and can affect the weight. A bowler holding the ball for the outswing delivery can fool the batsman because the ball ends up being an inswinger. The direction of the reverse swing is away from the rougher side, rather than towards it, as happens with a new ball.

RIGHT-ARM FINGER-SPINNER — An off-spin bowler who uses the first finger of the right hand to spin the ball from the off stump to the leg stump.

RIGHT-ARM WRIST-SPINNER — A leg-spinner who uses his wrist and three fingers on the right hand to turn the ball from the leg to the off.

ROLLER — A piece of equipment used by the ground staff to keep the pitch flat and ensure that it has a predictable and even bounce when the ball hits it. Some rollers are hand pulled (light roller); others are mechanically operated (heavy roller).

The roller is used on the pitch for different reasons. In the initial match preparation of a pitch, the ground staff will spend hours and hours rolling the pitch to get rid of any undulations and make the playing surface level. The heavy roller, sometimes machine-driven, is used. As the match progresses, the batting captain may be given the choice of the heavy or the light roller. The heavy roller will kill any grass and bring any moisture to the surface. It is often used when the batting captain has a big advantage on the first innings and he wants to break the pitch up or make it crumble, so that, for the opposition, batting conditions may be difficult against the spin bowlers. The lighter roller is used to smooth the pitch and prepare it for better batting conditions.

ROLLING, SWEEPING, MOWING, WATERING AND REPAIRING THE FOOT HOLES OF THE PITCH: *Law 10*— The pitch cannot be rolled during the match, except before the start of each innings and of each day's play. The pitch can be swept and rolled for not more than seven minutes. Rolling must take place no more than 30 minutes before the start of play on each day.

The pitch and the outfield can also be mown under the supervision of the umpires before play begins on each day. The pitch can be watered only during the initial pitch preparation and never during the match.

The creases can be remarked whenever possible. The foot holes can be repaired at any time to ensure the surface is flat for the bowler in his delivery stride. Many of these repairs take place before the start of play, when quick-set fillings or the replacement of turf can be used if necessary.

ROUND THE WICKET — A bowler delivering the ball from the right-hand side of the wickets, with the bowling arm being further away from the wickets at delivery.

RUBBER — A series of test matches. Now also relates to a series of one-day internationals.

RUBBERS — A colloquial term for rubber-soled boots or shoes.

RUN — A method of scoring by the batting team. A run or runs are scored from the bat or off the batsman's body. They also include extras such as wides and no balls, which are automatically credited to the batting team, and byes.

RUNNER — If a player is injured while fielding or when he is batting, another of his team mates can run between the wickets for him while he continues to bat. When the injured batsman is on strike, the runner will be positioned near the square leg umpire. When the other batsman takes strike, the runner will be at the non-striker's end. The runner can be run out, as can the injured batsman, if either one is out of his ground.

RUN OUT: Law 38 — A batsman is run out when the ball is in play and he fails to make his ground at either end of the pitch and the stumps have been broken. A batsman can also be run out off a no ball.

RUN THE BALL — In batting, to open the face of the bat and let the ball slide off and run down to third man.

RUN THE BALL AWAY — In bowling, to make the ball move away from the batsman, either in the air with swing or off the pitch with seam or cut.

RUN-UP — Steps taken by the bowler before he delivers the ball. A fast bowler will have a long run-up measuring 20 metres or more, while a spin bowler's run-up will be only a few paces or steps. The run-up is designed to give the bowler momentum and, when he gets to the crease to deliver the ball, it will have helped him get balance and poise at the time of ball release.

SANDSHOE-CRUSHER — A colloquial term for a yorker, derived from the possibility that the ball may hit the batsman's foot. Also known as a toe-crusher.

SCOOP — A type of cricket bat with one or more scoops cut out of the back to help distribute the weight and balance throughout the blade. The batsman can scoop the ball by getting the bat under the ball to hit it into the air.

SCORE — The state of the game in terms of runs scored and wickets taken in the scorebook and on the scoreboard, e.g. three wickets down for 250 runs. Also refers to a batsman's individual score.

SCOREBOARD — All first-class venues will have a large scoreboard on the ground that gives the players and the spectators all the information needed about the game. It will show the batsmen's runs, how they were dismissed, the fall of wickets, the bowlers' runs conceded and wickets captured, the extras and the team totals. Some club teams have a small portable scoreboard that shows only the team total, wickets lost and the last man's score or the overs that have been bowled.

SCORECARD — The printed match details that are sold at the ground on the morning of the match. Usually applies to county and test matches in England.

SCORER: *Law 4* — All games need two scorers to record every ball that has been bowled. Each team will provide a scorer and they will check at regular intervals to make sure that both books tally. The scorers will also acknowledge that they have received and understood the umpire's signals by waving or using a light.

SCORING: *Law 18* — After every ball has been bowled, the result of that ball will be entered into the scorebook. Entries include runs scored, maiden balls bowled, how out, fall of wickets and extras scored. Other matters will be recorded, including the day and date of the match, the names of the two teams, the venue of the match, who won the toss, the names of the umpires, the times when a batsman goes out to bat and when he is dismissed. The batsmen's runs, plus the extras (no balls, wides, leg byes and byes) must be the same as the bowlers' runs conceded, leg byes, and byes (wides and no balls count against the bowlers). The two totals must balance. (See Chapter 10.)

SEAM — This is where the four leather pieces (four-piece ball) or the two leather pieces (two-piece ball) are stitched together. Four raised rows of stitching go around the ball and the bowler's fingers grip the ball on, across or down the seam, depending on the type of bowler.

SEAMER OR SEAM BOWLING — A bowler, usually a medium-pace bowler who grips the ball down the seam of the ball or cuts his fingers across the seam and moves the ball off the pitch. He bowls either the leg-cutter or the off-cutter.

SELECTOR — A person who is officially appointed to pick or select the team. He may have other selectors on a panel to assist him. Players selected need to have ability, current form, fitness, potential and be able to adjust to the team culture and disciplines.

SEND BACK — When a batsman refuses, either by voice or signal, to respond to his partner's call for a run and the latter is sent back to his crease.

SERIES — Relates to the number of test or one-day matches between two countries contested in one meeting.

SESSION — A session is one of the three official periods of play throughout the day: the start of play to lunch, lunch to tea, and tea to the close of play.

SHAPE — A colloquial term for ball movement when it leaves the bowler's hand; for example, a ball may be described as having 'good shape'.

SHEFFIELD SHIELD — The trophy played for in Australia between the state teams in first-class cricket.

SHELL CUP — The trophy played for by all New Zealand first-class provincial sides in one-day cricket.

SHELL TROPHY — The trophy played for by all New Zealand first-class provinces in three- or four-day cricket.

SHINE — All fast bowlers like to have the shine on the ball because it helps the ball swing in the air. The shine retains the smooth, polished surface the ball had when new. Fielders will often shine the ball as the bowler walks back to his mark, often rubbing the ball vigorously on their trousers.

SHOOTER — A ball which, instead of bouncing off the pitch, shoots along the ground. This type of ball is very difficult for the batsman to combat because it takes him unawares. The batsman is sometimes dismissed lbw or bowled from one of these deliveries.

SHORT LEG — This is a close fielder on the leg side, usually 5 to 10 metres from the bat. Depending on where he finally stands, he could be short leg, backward short leg or forward short leg.

SHORT OF A LENGTH — A ball bowled, usually defensively, to force the batsman onto the back foot and prevent him scoring. If the ball is bowled straight, the batsman has to defend, but if the ball is pitched wide of the stumps the batsman may attempt to score runs with cut shots.

SHORT RUN — When a batsman doesn't make his ground at one end and turns for another run, the umpire will call 'One short' and signal to the scorers. The run is disallowed.

SHOT — A stroke played by the batsman.

SHOULDER ARMS — When the batsman offers no shot at a ball pitched outside the off stump and his bat is lifted above his shoulders.

SIDE — A cricket team or II (XI).

SIGHT-SCREENS — The white or sometimes very pale green or pale blue boarding placed on the boundary line behind the bowler's arm so that the batsman has a clear sight of the ball. For one-day cricket, played with a white ball, the sight-screen is black.

SIGNALS — The umpire will signal to the scorers with hand and arm motions for the start of play, byes, leg byes, no balls, wides, boundary fours/sixes, to cancel the previous decision, one short and to call the third umpire to view the video replay.

SILLY — Refers to catching positions very close to the batsman either on the leg side or the off side, known as silly mid-on or silly mid-off or bat-pad.

SINGLE (RUN) — One run scored by the batsman.

SINGLE-WICKET CRICKET — Two players compete against each other with special rules about the duration of the game. Both players have the assistance of 10 other fieldsmen.

SITTER — A fieldsman dropping an easy catch.

SIX-A-SIDE CRICKET — A form of cricket in which there are six players in each team, with special rules about the duration of the game. Usually each player except the wicket-keeper bowls at least one over if it is a five-over match or two overs each in a 10-over contest. In some matches a batsman may have to retire when he reaches a certain score, e.g. 30 runs.

SIX RUNS — Six runs are scored by the batsman when the ball carries over the boundary line on the full. The umpire will call and signal six runs to the scorers by raising both arms.

SKIPPER — Colloquial term for the captain.

SKITTLE — To comprehensively bowl out by hitting the wickets.

SKY — To hit the ball into the air. Sometimes described as a batsman 'skying the ball'.

SLASH — A batsman flaying with a cross-bat motion to a ball outside the off stump.

SLEDGE — A colloquial term used for abusive words directed at an opponent.

SLICE — A stroke made by the batsman on the off side, with the face of the bat unduly open, usually causing the ball to be hit high in the air.

SLINGER — Usually a pace bowler, whose slightly round-armed delivery compares with that of a javelin thrower, it is a 'slingshot' action. Jeff Thomson, the Australian fast bowler, is a good example.

SLIPPERY — A colloquial term for a bowler of pace who, in certain conditions, is difficult to face.

SLIPS — The fieldsmen positioned next to the wicket-keeper. When a fast bowler is operating there may be three slips in position — first, second and third. They are there to catch batsmen out because the ball sometimes slips or slides off the edge of the bat or is nicked by the batsman. They need very quick reflexes, excellent concentration and a safe pair of hands. These are regarded as prestigious specialist positions.

SLOG — A colloquial term for a batsman who hits across the line of the ball and tries to hit most of the balls faced to the boundary. These shots are sometimes called 'cow shots'.

SLOGGER — Usually a lower order batsman who plays aggressively and tries to hit boundaries. Some of the stroke play is unorthodox and adventurous; many shots are hits across the line of the ball, heaved away to mid-wicket or to the wide mid-on regions on the leg side.

SLOW BOWLER — Usually, a bowler who attempts to deceive the batsman with flight or spin.

SNICK — When the ball just hits the outside edge of the bat on its way past the batsman.

SPILL A CATCH — The fieldsman or wicket-keeper has dropped a catch, allowing the batsman to continue his innings.

SPIN — A ball from a slow bowler that hits the pitch and turns either way.

SPIN BOWLER — A slow bowler who spins the ball off the pitch. There are several types of spin bowlers including right-arm off-spin, right-arm leg-spin and left-arm orthodox. Spin bowlers are either termed finger- or wrist-spinners, depending on their specialty.

SPLICE — The V-shaped cut at the top of the bat where the handle is attached. When the ball hits that area, it is said to have 'spliced the bat'.

SPONGY WICKET — The grass roots are long and, when cut, the grass remains on the pitch, making it soft. The ball is gripped by the grass, so that it bounces more sharply and spins more than expected.

SPRIGS — Metal spikes on boots or shoes that prevent players slipping.

SQUARE CUT — A stroke to a ball that has pitched short and wide of the offstump. The batsman moves his back foot across to the off stump and hits down over the top of the ball by rolling his wrists over it. The ball is hit between the cover point and the gully area towards third man.

SQUARE LEG — A fielding position on the on side, square of the wicket about 20 metres behind the batsman.

STAND-BY PLAYERS — When a team has been selected, several other players may be advised that they are on stand-by in case a player becomes unavailable through injury or illness, etc. Stand-by players are required to retain their fitness and continue practising in case they get called up.

START OF PLAY: *Law 15* — Each match starts at an agreed time. The umpires call 'Play' at the start of any session, and on the resumption of play after any interruption,

STATE — Refers to the condition of the pitch, or to the stage of play.

STATISTICS — The game of cricket is about figures. Batting and bowling statistics are recorded after every match so that players know exactly what they have or haven't achieved in the game or throughout the season. Batting and bowling averages determine how effective players are and what rating they may have.

STICKS — A slang term for the wickets or stumps.

STICKY WICKET — A wicket or pitch that has been affected by rain and starts to dry out in the sunshine, turning into a glue pot. The surface of the pitch firms up but underneath it remains damp, causing the ball to bite into the pitch, and turn and bounce sharply. Batting is very difficult.

STOCK BALL — The usual ball a bowler delivers during an over, e.g. the outswinger or the inswinger.

STOCK BOWLER — A bowler who is asked to bowl tightly and prevent batsmen scoring runs. He will bowl 20 or more overs in the day and if he has figures of 2/40, he has done a good job for the team.

STOLEN SINGLE — A batsman has taken a daring run that he would not normally have taken. It is also called a 'risky single' and, if the batsman was run out, would be termed 'a stupid run'.

STONEWALLER — A batsman who is difficult to get out because he is all defence and takes no risks. He plays a lot of dead bat shots at the ball.

STRIKE — A batsman hitting the ball with the bat. Also refers to the batsman facing a bowler, i.e. taking strike.

STRIKER — The batsman who is facing or receiving the ball from the bowler.

STRIKE RATE — A player's batting rate is measured by the number of runs scored per 100 balls faced. In bowling, it is the number of balls bowled for each wicket taken.

STUMPED: *Law 39* — A batsman is out stumped when, on receiving the ball, he is out of his ground when the wicket-keeper breaks the wickets with the ball in hand or if the ball rebounds off the wicket-keeper's body onto the wickets. A wicket-keeper cannot take the ball in front of the wickets for a stumping unless the ball has touched the bat or batsman first. A batsman can be stumped off a wide ball — this is unusual and if it happens the batting team gets an extra run for the wide.

STUMPS: *Law 8* — A set of three wooden wickets is positioned at each end of the pitch. The sets of wickets are 22.86 centimetres (9 inches) wide and two wooden bails are placed on the top of each set. The distance between the two sets of wickets is 20.12 metres (22 yards). The wickets should stand 71.1 centimetres (28 inches) above the ground. (See diagram on p. 76.)

STUMPS ARE DRAWN — At the scheduled close of play and when the last over of the day has been completed, the umpires will call 'Time' and pull the stumps out of the ground.

SUBSTITUTES: *Law 2.1* — Usually, the twelfth man or a specialist fielder who takes the field of play for an injured or incapacitated player is called a substitute. He can only act as a fielder and cannot bat or bowl. The opposing captain must be asked before the substitute can take the field.

SUNDRIES — See 'extras'.

SWEEPER — A fieldsman positioned on the boundary, usually square on the off side on the cover boundary or the on side at deep backward square. His job is to cover a large area by roaming or sweeping backwards and forwards. These fielders are fast and have a very good throwing arm.

SWEEP SHOT — A stroke played by the batsman to a ball pitching outside the leg stump and turning further away. The batsman extends his front leg towards the line of the ball while the back leg kneels on the ground. The bat sweeps the ball around to the leg side with the roll of the wrists. It is usually played to an off-spin bowler and hit downwards. It is also played against a leg-spin bowler but this is regarded as a dangerous shot because the batsman is hitting across the line of the spin instead of sweeping with it.

SWERVE/SHAPE/SWING — A term used for a ball that moves or curves in the air. It is an inswinger or an outswinger.

SWING — A ball that moves in the air: an inswinger or an outswinger.

SWING BOWLER — A bowler who has the ability to move the ball in the air, whether it is an inswinger or an outswinger.

SWORD — A colloquial term to describe the bat.

TAIL — That part of the batting order which is at the end of the innings. These players are usually specialist bowlers or the wicket-keeper, who have less skill with the bat. They are not expected to score many runs — some are rabbits and ferrets. Some 'tails' are said to wag when the batsmen excel and score useful runs.

TAIL-ENDER — Usually the last batsman in the batting order although numbers nine, 10 and 11 are regarded as tail-enders. The terms rabbit and ferret apply to these batsmen.

TEA BREAK — Twenty minutes are allowed for a tea break. The actual time that is taken will vary from match to match. The umpires need to be aware that if the scheduled tea break is, for example, at 3.40 p.m. and the batting team has lost nine wickets, play will continue for a further 30 minutes or until the fall of the tenth wicket, whichever is the earliest.

TESTIMONIAL SEASON — Also called a benefit season, awarded to a player who has given good and loyal service to a club, usually over a 10-year period. The player can form a committee and organise fund-raising activities to secure his future when he retires from the game. Activities include dinners, auctions, raffles, golf days, cricket matches, etc.

TEST MATCH — A match played by two countries who are full representatives of the ICC. These are Australia, Bangladesh, England, India, New Zealand, Pakistan, South Africa, Sri Lanka, West Indies and Zimbabwe. The games are played over five days, usually over a three-match series but in some cases over five matches, e.g. the Ashes between England and Australia. There are also one-off tests followed by a one-day series.

THIGHPAD — A pad worn by the batsman to protect the thigh area of the body. For a right-handed batsman, the thighpad is positioned above the batting pads on the left or the front leading leg. For a left-handed batsman, the thighpad is worn on the right leg.

THIRD MAN — A fielding position close to the boundary on the off side in between the slips and the gully.

THIRD UMPIRE — In international matches and some other forms of cricket, the umpires in the middle can ask for a video replay of an incident, e.g run out, stumping, catch, whether the ball was hit for a six or a four. The third umpire will view the replay and advise the umpires in the middle of the correct decision.

THREE FOR, TWO FOR — Players' terms used when a bowler has captured three wickets or two wickets. Instead of saying, for example, 3-43 or 2-40, the bowler has 'three for'.

THROW/THROWING — A fielder will return the ball to the wicket-keeper or to the fielder behind the stumps at the bowler's end, using an overarm or underarm throw. The ball is thrown overarm from the boundary because it will get to its destination quickly. The underarm throw is from a short distance when the fielder picks the ball up in one hand and fires it at the wickets or to the fielder behind the stumps.

Law 24.3 —Throwing also relates to the no ball law, where a bowler must bowl the ball and not throw it. Once the bowler's arm has reached shoulder level in the delivery swing, the elbow joint must not be straightened either partially or completely until the ball has left the hand otherwise either umpire shall call 'No ball'.

THROW DOWNS — Before the start of a match or at practice a batsman may ask to have some throw downs. Another team member will bowl so the batsman can practise timing and gain confidence.

TICKLE — A faint edge off the bat by the batsman to a ball going down and outside the leg stump, with the ball going to fine leg for runs.

TIE — A test or first-class match is tied when the team batting second have lost all their 10 wickets and the accumulated runs of both teams are the same. There is no winner or loser. In a one-day match, if the scores are equal, irrespective of wickets lost, the match is tied.

TIMBERS — A colloquial term for the stumps or wickets.

TIME — In batting this refers to a player who appears to have more time than most to get into position to play a shot at the ball, whether it is a defensive or an attacking one. Also refers to a batsman timing his shot and hitting the ball well. Umpires also call 'Time' at the end of play.

TIMED OUT: *Law 31* — An incoming batsman can be timed out when he wilfully takes more than two minutes to come to the wicket. The time is measured from the fall of a wicket to the moment the batsman steps onto the field of play. The umpire must be sure that the delay was wilful and if there is an appeal from the fielding team, the umpire at the bowler's end is obliged to give the batsman out. This form of dismissal is very rare.

TIME WASTING: *Law 42.10* — Deliberate time wasting is unfair to the other team. The fielding team can slow the over rate down so that the batting team cannot face extra balls, e.g. the bowler walks slowly back to his bowling mark and takes too long to bowl an over. An over should be completed in between three and four minutes. The fielding captain may alter his field several times during an over to slow the over rate down. Sometimes the batsman will spend time gardening and delay the time before he takes strike again. These delaying tactics to prevent the other team winning are not in the spirit of the game and the umpire can step in and warn the players. They can be reported to the authority controlling the game.

TOE — The bottom edge of the bat.

TON — A slang term used when a batsman scores a century or a hundred.

TONK — A slog shot. A batsman who regularly plays this way is known as a 'tonker'.

TOP SPIN — This is spin that helps the ball gain pace off the pitch when it hits the ground and then continues on the same line. Usually bowled by the wrist-spinner, although the off-spinner can use this to good effect because the ball does not spin.

TOSS FOR INNINGS — Before the start of play both captains meet, usually in the middle of the pitch, declare their teams to each other in writing, and one captain will toss a coin while the other will call either 'Heads' or 'Tails'. The captain winning the toss decides whether to bat or bowl first.

TRACK — A slang term for the pitch or wicket. A batsman is sometimes said 'to have gone down the track to get to the pitch of the ball'.

TROT — A colloquial term for a sequence of runs when the batsmen amble through easily. Also applied to a player having a good or bad run of form, i.e. 'a good trot' or 'a bad trot'.

TURN — Another term for spin off the pitch by a slow or spin bowler.

TWEAKER — Another term for a spin bowler, usually a leg-spin bowler who tweaks the ball from his fingers and the wrist.

TWELFTH MAN — This is the reserve or extra player who acts as a substitute fieldsman when a fellow team member is incapacitated for any reason, such as injury or illness. He can only take the field of play as a substitute with the approval of the opposing captain. He cannot bat or bowl. Usually he brings the drinks onto the field of play and acts as the team's general dogsbody.

TWIST — This is the act of spinning the ball by a spin bowler. It is the same as tweak.

TWO-PACED WICKET — A pitch surface that has patches of varying turf, where the ball bounces differently. In some cases the pitch may have a hard and soft surface and the ball behaves in an unpredictable manner.

TWO RUNS — Two runs are scored by the batsmen when they cross twice and secure their ground at each end. The batsman facing the bowler is credited with the runs.

UMPIRES (INCLUDING THE THIRD UMPIRE): *Law 3* — The two umpires appointed for the match have a big responsibility but should not interfere with play unless the spirit of the game or the Laws of Cricket are broken. They cannot be changed during the match unless both captains agree. Before the match starts they should advise the captains of any special rules or conditions that will apply; e.g. the hours of play, the official clock by which time is judged, the choice of balls that can be used and any local rules affecting the boundary. They will also make sure the wickets or stumps are pitched and that all the instruments of play, such as the stumps and bats, conform to the laws. An umpire can change his decision and should do so quicidy if he feels a genuine mistake has been made.

The third umpire, used in international matches only, sits in a room in the stand, watching the game on a television monitor with no sound. When the third umpire is called into action by the umpires in the middle, he will be asked to adjudicate on whether the batsman is out (bowled, stumped, run out or caught), whether a four or six has been scored or whether the fielder has come into contact with the boundary line while touching the ball. The third umpire has become an accepted part of the game.

UNDERARM — In bowling, to deliver the ball with the bowling arm coming through below the shoulder. This is now an unacceptable form of bowling. In fielding, to throw underarm to shy at the stumps.

UNDERSPIN — A term for back-spin. The fingers come straight down behind the back of the ball during release. Medium-pace bowlers use this method to keep the seam of the ball upright during its flight. Some of the slower bowlers use the thumb to obtain back-spin and flatten the flight of the ball. The ball will sometimes cut off the pitch, creating problems for the batsman.

UNFAIR PLAY: *Law 42* — The captains must ensure that the game is played in the true spirit and within the Laws of Cricket. The umpires will intervene if they feel that these are contravened in any way. This will include player sledging, players damaging the pitch, persistent short-pitched bowling, bowling head-high deliveries, doctoring the ball, time wasting, obstructing the field or obstructing the batsman.

UNPLAYABLE DELIVERY — Sometimes called a jaffer or a UPN (unplayable nut). This is the perfect delivery from a bowler, which completely deceives and beats the batsman.

UPRIGHTS — A colloquial term used for the wickets or stumps.

USE THE CREASE — In bowling, to vary the delivery position in relation to the stumps and the batting and return crease.

USE YOUR FEET — In batting against spin bowlers, to leave the crease in an attempt to smother the spin of the ball or to get to the pitch of the ball and hit it with an attacking stroke.

VICE-CAPTAIN — The second-in-command, or deputy, who takes over if the captain is injured, leaves the field of play, or is otherwise unavailable. The captain may consult the vice-captain when making a difficult decision.

WALK — The batsman will sometimes walk back to the pavilion, without waiting for the umpire's decision, if he knows he has hit the ball and it has been fairly caught by the fielding team. This happens in the spirit of fair play, but most batsmen will wait for the umpire to make the decision.

WET WICKET or PITCH — A pitch affected by rain, causing the ball to leave the pitch slowly. When the ball pitches, it will take a divot out of the turf or pitch and the batsman will repair it.

This type of pitch becomes pitted when wet and the indentations allow the seam bowlers to prosper as it dries.

WHOPPER — A colloquial term to describe a big hit by a batsman.

WICKET-KEEPER: *Law 40* — The wicket-keeper must remain behind the stumps until the ball delivered by the bowler has reached the bat, batsman, passes the wickets or until the batsman sets off for a run. If the wicket-lseeper contravenes the law, the square leg umpire will call 'No ball'. The wicket-keeper is the only fieldsman who may wear gloves and he also wears protective pads. He also supports the bowler in lbw appeals and assists the captain in setting the field and getting the angles right. He will also help the bowler decide what line and length to bowl and can analyse the batsman's technique because he is in the best position to see.

WICKET MAIDEN — This occurs when a bowler concedes no runs from the bat and dismisses a batsman in the same over.

WICKETS: *Law 8* — Also known as the stumps. A set of three wickets is positioned at each end of the pitch, 20.12 metres (22 yards) apart. Each set of stumps is 22.86 centimetres (9 inches) wide, and they stand 71.1 centimetres (28 inches) above the ground. A set of two bails sits on top of the three stumps. (See diagram on p. 76.)

WICKETS ARE DOWN: *Law 28* — The wickets are down when a ball falls to the ground. Either the ball, a fielder with the ball in hand or the batsman's bat or part of his person, including his hat falling off, can cause the bail to fall. When the wickets are down, the fielding team can appeal to the umpire for a possible dismissal, either bowled, run out, stumped or hit wicket. If the wind blows the bails off the wickets, the umpires will call 'Dead ball'. The bails will be put back on top of the stumps and play will continue.

WIDE BALL: *Law 25* — A wide ball is bowled so high or wide of the batsman that, in the opinion of the umpire, he cannot hit it. A wide counts as on run to the batting team and the ball has to be bowled again. If the wide ball beats the wicket-keeper and goes over the boundary line, it will be recorded as four wides. The umpire will signal to the scorers and call 'Wide'.

A batsman can be stumped off a wide ball but the batting team will be credited with an extra run.

WINSOR CUP — A special award presented to the New Zealand bowler who has achieved the most meritorious bowling performances in first-class matches since the award was last made.

WISDEN — This is cricket's 'Bible'. A yearly publication recording details of every test, first-class and one-day match, and any other important games during that year. *Wisden* was first published in 1864 by the Sussex cricketer John Wisden. It also contains a record of obituaries, the Laws of Cricket, player statistics, photographs and other useful information.

WOOD — A colloquial term for the bat. 'To get some wood on it' means to edge the ball or make some contact with the bat.

WOODWORK — A colloquial term for the stumps or wickets.

WRIST-SPINNER — A leg-spin bowler who spins the ball by rotating the wrist.

WRONG 'UN — A slang term for a googly. A ball bowled by a right-arm leg-spinner that gives the impression of being a leg-spinner but spins the other or wrong way.

YOBBO (YABBA) — A spectator who becomes unruly and boisterous, calling obscenities to the players, directed usually at the opposition. Yabba was the infamous Australian barracker who yelled out to visiting teams to try and upset their concentration. Some comments, however, were quite humorous, e.g. to the batsman who was playing dead bat shots at the ball and boring the crowd, Yabba yelled out, 'Bowl him a piano and see if he can play that.'

YORKER — In bowling, a delivery that passes under the bat, having pitched very full in length. Generally, a bowler may york a batsman but he cannot positively bowl a yorker. The batsman tends to york himself when he tries to play a full toss as a half volley, or a half volley as a full toss, eventually missing the ball, which goes under the bat, and sometimes bowls the batsman out. If the batsman successfully gets bat on ball and digs it out, the commentator may say, 'The bowler has tried to york the batsman.'

CHAPTER 21

Cricket Trivia
100 Cricket Questions

QUESTIONS
1. Who was the first batsman to score 5000 test runs?
2. Who was the first player to make 100 consecutive test appearances?
3. Who was the first player to score a test century batting as a night-watchman?
4. Which two countries took part in the 1000th test match?
5. Which English off-spin bowler took four wickets in six balls in a test match in 1965?
6. Which Indian leg-spinner took a record-breaking 16 wickets on his test debut in 1988?
7. Who is the only test player never to have batted, bowled, or taken a catch?
8. Who holds the test record for scoring the most centuries in consecutive test matches?
9. Who were the only two batsmen to score double-centuries in the World Series Cricket 'super tests'?
10. Who was the first batsman to score more than 200 runs in boundaries in a test match?
11. Who scored over 4000 runs in first-class cricket in 1987?
12. Don Bradman was the first batsman to score 25 test centuries. Who was the first batsman to score 50 test half-centuries?

13. Which England batsman captained his country at both cricket and soccer?
14. Who was the New Zealand batsman who played a rugby international for England in 1947?
15. For which other country has the West Indian opening batsman Desmond Haynes played?
16. Who is the only player to have scored more than 55,000 runs and captured 2000 wickets in first-class cricket?
17. When was the eight-ball over last used in Australian first-class cricket?
18. What was so unusual about the cricket team that toured England in 1874?
19. Who was the first South African bowler to take 100 test wickets?
20. Who was the first player to complete the all-round feat of 1000 runs, 100 wickets and 100 catches in test cricket?
21. Which Pakistani batsman was given out 'handled ball' during the first test against Australia in Karachi in 1982 ?
22. Who batted in 57 test innings against Australia and was never dismissed for a duck?
23. Who took a record amount of time (97 minutes) to get off the mark in the fourth test at Adelaide in 1946-47?
24. Who was the first player to score a century and take five wickets in the same one-day international?
25. Who captained New Zealand to their first ever test victory?
26. On which ground is the Kirkstall Lane end?
27. In how many test countries did Don Bradman play?
28. What was Bradman's highest test score as captain?
29. What was Ian Botham's highest score in first-class cricket?
30. Dubbed 'Peter Who' by the press, he took eight wickets, scored 53 runs and was named man of the match. Who was he?
31. Who was the Australian batsman dismissed first ball on his

test debut in 1985 against England at Leeds?
32. Who did India beat to win their first ever test?
33. Who was the first man to play a test for two different countries?
34. Wnich England player was no balled for throwing in a test match in 1986?
35. Which New Zealand player ended up in hospital after being felled by a bouncer from Peter Lever at Auckland in 1975?
36. Which country batted through its second innings in a test match in 1976 with five batsmen absent because of injury?
37. Who was the Pakistani umpire involved in a heated on-field dispute with the England captain Mike Gatting, at Faisalabad in 1987?
38. Which West Indian fast bowler caused controversy when he barged into umpire Fred Goodall at Lancaster Park, Christchurch in 1980?
39. Who stumped three batsmen in a hat trick?
40. Which 17-year-old school boy dismissed eight batsmen on his first-class debut in 1981?
41. Who was the first wicket-keeper to take more than 20 catches in a five-match test series in Australia?
42. Where was cricket prohibited by law in 1890?
43. Which player made 71 consecutive test appearances for Australia?
44. Who was the first South African batsman to score 10,000 runs in Currie Cup cricket?
45. Who was the first batsman in New Zealand Plunket Shield cricket to score two triple centuries?
46. Who was the first Antiguan cricketer to play test cricket for the West Indies?
47. Who bowled Don Bradman for a duck in his last test innings?

48. Which two fielders have taken three catches in a hat trick?
49. Which West Indian batsman made four 100s in test cricket before his 21st birthday?
50. Who was recalled to the England test team at the age of 45 for the 1976 test series against the West Indies?
51. Who is the youngest batsman to have scored a triple test century?
52. List eight ways a batsman can be dismissed.
53. What is the penalty if a fielder stops the ball with his cap?
54. Can an injured batsman be run out if his runner is out of his crease?
55. How can a batsman be timed out?
56. When does a ball cease to be dead?
57. Which famous England cricketer told Victor Trumper, when he was a lad, that 'he would never make a batsman'?
58. Apart from being test cricketers, what do Dennis Lillee and Dr. W. G. Grace have in common?
59. Which two non-playing test nations took part in the 1975 World Cup in England?
60. Who scored a match-winning 175* in the 1983 World Cup match against Zimbabwe when his team was 5 for 17?
61. Which West Indian fast bowler took a record-breaking 7 wickets for 51 against Australia in the 1983 World Cup?
62. Who was the first bowler to capture a hat trick in the World Cup?
63. Who has most often achieved the double of scoring 1000 runs and capturing 100 wickets in the same season during England's first-class county cricket season?
64. Whose first scoring shot in test cricket was a six off the bowling of Ian Botham?
65. Who was the first Australian opening batsman to be run out twice in the same test match?

66. Who captained New Zealand to their first test win on Australian soil?
67. Name John Wright's 10 opening batting partners in test cricket.
68. How many New Zealand test players have had surnames starting with W?
69. Which New Zealand provincial team did Ken Rutherford play for?
70. How many test wickets did Kapil Dev capture?
71. Who won the 1996 World Cup, held in India and Pakistan?
72. Where was the world's 50th test venue?
73. Who scored a 100 in each innings of the test at Auckland in 1978 between New Zealand and England?
74. How many first-class wickets did Wilfred Rhodes capture?
75. Aravinda De Silva plays for which country?
76. Who holds the record for most test runs?
77. Who did Zimbabwe beat in 1995 to win their first ever test match?
78. Who is the only player to take 11 wickets and score 50 or more in a test match at Lord's?
79. When Brian Lara scored a world record 501 runs in an innings, whose record did he beat?
80. How many first-class 100s did Jack Hobbs score?
81. Who was the first bowler to capture 300 test wickets!
82. What is the highest test score made by a New Zealand batsman?
83. Who is the only New Zealand bowler to capture a hat trick in test cricket?
84. Who is the only batsman to score centuries in each of his first three tests?
85. Who scored 18 and 1 in his first test, was dropped next test but then went on to score nearly 7000 test runs?

86. Who scored 259 for New Zealand in a test during the West Indies tour in 1971?
87. Who scored 1001 test runs and took 102 test wickets for New Zealand?
88. Who bowled the first ball in test cricket between Australia and England on 15 March 1877?
89. How many runs did Martin Donnelly score for New Zealand at Lord's in 1949?
90. How many New Zealand batsmen whose surnames start with H have scored test centuries since 1946?
91. Who was the England batsman run out at the bowler's end by Ewen Chatfield during the test match at Lancaster Park, Christchurch in 1978?
92. Who had the highest individual test score before Brian Lara's 375 broke the record?
93. How old was James Southerton of England when he played his first test in 1877?
94. What do the following players have in common: Len Hutton, Mike Brearley, Glenn Turner, Ken Barrington and Graham Gooch?
95. What English county cricket team did Clive Rice play for?
96. Who won the English County Championship in 1987?
97. Who were the first father and son to each capture 100 test wickets?
98. Who had the nickname Deadly in test cricket?
99. How many first-class wickets did Ewen Chatfield capture?
100. Which Fijian batsman was good enough to score more than 1000 runs on the 1948 tour of New Zealand?

ANSWERS

1. Jack Hobbs (England).
2. Sunil Gavaskar (Bombay 1974-75, Madras 1985-86).
3. Nasim Ul Ghani (Pakistan v England at Lord's in 1962).
4. Pakistan and New Zealand at Hyderabad in 1984-85.
5. Fred Titmus (England v New Zealand at Leeds).
6. Narenda Hirwani (16-136, India v West Indies at Madras).
7. Jack MacBryan (England).
8. Don Bradman (Australia) 6: 270, 212, 169, 144*, 102*, 103.
9. Barry Richards (World) (207) and Greg Chappell (Australia) (246*).
10. John Edrich (England v New Zealand at Leeds, 1965).
11. Martin Crowe (New Zealand).
12. Len Hutton (England).
13. 'Tip' Foster.
14. Martin Donnelly.
15. Scotland.
16. Frank Woolley (England).
17. 1978-79.
18. It was an American baseball team, which also played cricket.
19. Neil Adcock.
20. Garfield Sobers (West Indies).
21. Mohsin Khan.
22. John Edrich (England).
23. Godfrey Evans (England).
24. Viv Richards, 119 and 5-41 (West Indies v New Zealand at Dunedin in 1987).
25. John Reid.

26. Headingley (Leeds, England).
27. Two (England and Australia).
28. 295 (Australia v England at Melbourne in 1936-37).
29. 228 (Somerset v Gloucestershire at Taunton in 1980).
30. Peter Taylor (Australia).
31. Simon O'Donnell.
32. England (by an innings and eight runs).
33. Billy Midwinter (Australia/England).
34. David Gower (England v New Zealand at Trent Bridge in 1986
35. Ewen Chatfield.
36. India (v West Indies at Kingston, Jamaica).
37. Shakoor Rana.
38. Colin Croft.
39. W. H. Brain (off C.L. Townsend, Gloucestershire v Somerset at Cheltenham in 1893).
40. Jack Russell (Gloucestershire v Sri Lanka at Bristol).
41. Steve Rixon (22 v India 1977-78).
42. Samoa.
43. Ian Chappell.
44. Graeme Pollock.
45. Bert Sutcliffe (355 v Auckland at Dunedin in 1949 and 385 v Canterbury at Lancaster Park, Christchurch in 1952-53).
46. Andy Roberts (1974).
47. Eric Hollies (England).
48. George Thompson from the bowling of S.G. Smith (Northamptonshire v Warwickshire at Birmingham, England, 1914) and Cyril White off R. Beesley (Border v Griqualand West at Border, South Africa, 1946~7).
49. George Headley.
50. Brian Close.

51. Garfield Sobers (21 years 216 days, 365* — West Indies v Pakistan at Kingston, Jamaica, 1957-58).
52. Bowled, caught, lbw, run out, stumped, handled the ball, hit the ball twice, obstruction, timed out, hit wicket.
53. Five runs shall be added to any runs already taken, including the run in progress, if the batsmen have crossed. If the batsman has hit the ball, he shall receive the benefit of the runs, otherwise the extras will benefit.
54. Yes.
55. Upon an appeal by the fielding team at the fall of a wicket, the incoming batsman has two minutes to reach the field of play.
56. When the bowler begins his run-up or action.
57. W. G. Grace.
58. They share the same birthday, 18 July.
59. East Africa, Sri Lanka.
60. Kapil Dev (India v Zimbabwe at Tunbridge Wells, Kent).
61. Winston Davis.
62. Chetan Sharma (India v New Zealand at Nagpur, India, 1987).
63. Wilfred Rhodes (16 times).
64. Carlisle Best (West Indies v England at Kingston, Jamaica, 1986).
65. Mark Taylor (Australia v West Indies at Adelaide, 1988-89).
66. Jeremy Coney (1985-86 at the Gabba in Brisbane, Australia).
67. Robert Anderson, Bruce Edgar, Trevor Franklin, Geoff Howarth, Bert Vance, Ken Rutherford, Phil Home, Blair Hardand, Mark Greatbatch and Jeff Crowe.
68. Thirteen (Ken Wadsworth, Merv Wallace, Kerry Walmsley, John Ward, Willie Watson, Les Watt, Murray Webb, Peter Webb, G. Lindsay Weir, David White, Paul Whitelaw, John Wright, Paul Wiseman).
69. Otago.

70. 434.
71. Sri Lanka.
72. McLean Park, Napier, New Zealand.
73. Geoff Howarth (New Zealand).
74. 4187.
75. Sri Lanka.
76. Allan Border (Australia) —11,174 runs at an average of 50.56.
77. Pakistan.
78. Dion Nash (New Zealand).
79. Hanif Mohammad (Pakistan) (499).
80. 197.
81. Fred Trueman (England).
82. 299 (Martin Crowe, New Zealand v Sri Lanka at Wellington).
83. Peter Petherick (New Zealand v Pakistan at Lahore in 1976).
84. Mohammad Azharuddin (India).
85. Don Bradman.
86. Glenn Turner.
87. John Bracewell.
88. Alfred Shaw (England).
89. 206.
90. (Walter Hadlee, Richard Hadlee, P. G. Z. Harris, Brian Hastings, Geoffrey Howarth, Matthew Home).
91. Derek Randall.
92. Garfield Sobers (West Indies) (365).
93. 49.
94. They all scored a test duck on debut.
95. Nottinghamshire.
96. Nottinghamshire.
97. Lance and Chris Cairns.

98. Derek Underwood (Kent and England, accurate, left-arm orthodox spin bowler).
99. 587.
100. Ilikena Lasarusa Talebulamainelilikenamainavaleniveivakabulaimainakulalakeba. Better known as I.L. Bula.